WHY CAN'T I GET IT TOGETHER?

KICK UNREALISTIC
EXPECTATIONS TO THE CURB
AND REST IN GOD'S TRUTH

JAMIE IVEY

W PUBLISHING GROUP

AN IMPRINT OF THOMAS NELSON

Why Can't I Get It Together?

© 2024 Jamie Ivey

Published in Nashville, Tennessee, by W Publishing, an imprint of Thomas Nelson.

Author represented by Illuminate Literary Agency.

Thomas Nelson titles may be purchased in bulk for educational, business, fundraising, or sales promotional use. For information, please email SpecialMarkets@ ThomasNelson.com.

Unless otherwise noted, Scripture quotations are taken from the ESV® Bible (The Holy Bible, English Standard Version®). Copyright © 2001 by Crossway, a publishing ministry of Good News Publishers. Used by permission. All rights reserved.

Scripture quotations marked CSB are taken from the Christian Standard Bible®. Copyright © 2017 by Holman Bible Publishers. Used by permission. Christian Standard Bible® and CSB® are federally registered trademarks of Holman Bible Publishers.

Scripture quotations marked MSG are taken from THE MESSAGE. Copyright © 1993, 2002, 2018 by Eugene H. Peterson. Used by permission of NavPress. All rights reserved. Represented by Tyndale House Publishers, a division of Tyndale House Ministries.

Scripture quotations marked NIV are taken from the Holy Bible, New International Version®, NIV®. Copyright © 1973, 1978, 1984, 2011 by Biblica, Inc.® Used by permission of Zondervan. All rights reserved worldwide. www.zondervan.com. The "NIV" and "New International Version" are trademarks registered in the United States Patent and Trademark Office by Biblica, Inc.®

Scripture quotations marked NKJV are taken from the New King James Version®. Copyright © 1982 by Thomas Nelson. Used by permission. All rights reserved.

Scripture quotations marked NLT are taken from the Holy Bible, New Living Translation. Copyright © 1996, 2004, 2015 by Tyndale House Foundation. Used by permission of Tyndale House Ministries, Carol Stream, Illinois 60188. All rights reserved.

ISBN 978-1-4003-3394-3 (Audiobook)
ISBN 978-1-4003-3393-6 (ePub)
ISBN 978-1-4003-3392-9 (Softcover)

Library of Congress Cataloging-in-Publication Data

2023941248

Printed in the United States of America

23 24 25 26 27 LBC 5 4 3 2 1

To all the friends in my life who have helped me trust God in every season of my life, this is for you. You have lived out these words, and I'm better for it.

CONTENTS

PART III—SHAPING YOUR REALITY

PART IV—CELEBRATING YOUR FUTURE REALITY

INTRODUCTION

I'M HERE WITH YOU

"For the love, Jamie! Get yourself together," I declared aloud for no one to hear. No one except me.

Once again, I had failed at something. This time it was a scheduling issue. Like many people, I live and die by my calendar. I find great joy in how organized it is and can even get a bit prideful about that. But then when I forget something, I feel such shame and guilt.

On this day, I was supposed to be in two places at one time— doing something for work that had been scheduled *for* me and doing something personal that had been scheduled *by* me. I had booked something personal without checking to see if anything was booked for work. That meant I was going to disappoint someone. My options were either to cancel a work event, which would affect numerous people besides myself, or cancel on my daughter, which would affect only her—but she's the *last* person I want to disappoint.

I hate situations like this. I knew I had gotten myself into this, and I knew it was all my fault. I was trying to be everything to everyone, and it backfired on me.

I always thought that the older I got, the more I'd have my life in order. Have you thought that too? No matter how old we are, we tend to look at the next decade of life and declare, "*That* will be the decade I get myself together." We say things like:

- When I have a job, I'll be better with my finances.
- When I get a job I love, I'll work harder.
- When I find a loving relationship, I'll finally put the sexual abuse from my childhood behind me.
- When I get married, I'll stop wanting to look at porn.
- When my kids sleep through the night, I'll stop being angry in the morning.
- When my kids are off to college, I'll focus on my marriage.
- When I am not so stressed, I'll start taking care of my body.
- When I have more time in my day, I'll never double-book myself.

And yet we never do. We keep falling into the same traps. We often hide our fears or struggles because we are afraid of what others will think of us if they know the truth.[i] We try to pull ourselves up by our bootstraps over and over and over again. Still, we just can't ever seem to do it right.

From overscheduling to jealousy to daydreaming about another life—I don't want to do these things. *I know better.* I have learned the hard way. But I keep doing the same things I don't want to do.

One of my least favorite personal qualities is that I can be quite critical of the people who live in my house. I don't know why it's just toward them, but it is. If I had a dollar for all the mornings I've woken up and begged myself to be different than I was the morning

---

i. I wrote a whole book about this: *If You Only Knew: My Unlikely, Unavoidable Story of Becoming Free*. Check it out!

before, I'd have quite a few dollars in my wallet! It stems from my desire for control—I know it, and I hate it.

Not too long ago, I woke up determined to be a different mom that day. I am fully aware of my tendency to move toward criticism, and that day was going to be *different*. I was going to be positive! I was going to *not* focus on the negative things. I pumped myself up all morning. I prayed in the shower while shaving my legs. I listened to worship music while putting on my makeup. I even made my bed with a smile.[ii]

Then I walked downstairs.

The dog had pooped on the floor. Shoes were left all over the place from the night before. Someone was asking me to sign papers that had to be turned in *that day*. Oh—and they also needed twenty dollars in cash. And then, of course, there was a full-blown fight over the last everything bagel.[iii]

I began to sing the words, "God, I look to You, You're where my help comes from . . ." as I tried to maintain the attitude I had declared seconds earlier while in my quiet room talking to Jesus.[1] But within minutes, my theme song switched to "Jesus, Take the Wheel" as I begrudgingly picked up pair after pair of shoes, and then the dog poop, all while signing papers and giving my kids permission to do God-knows-what.[iv]

As the kids ran to catch the bus, I stood silently in the kitchen, recovering from my fourteen minutes of misery. What happened to *I'm going to be the best before-school-morning-mom ever*? Once again, I had failed and it was barely the start of my day.

---

ii. Let's be honest, a made bed can do miracles for a mood!

iii. I get the fight over the bagel. That "everything" stuff is what mornings are made for!

iv. I have no idea what I signed. Watching R-rated movies at school? Going on a school trip to Japan? I have no clue. I just signed it.

While this is a common parenting struggle for me, you likely have your own issues. Life seems to be continually three steps forward and two steps backward for us all, no matter what season we find ourselves in.

Think through your day—just yesterday and today. Are there moments when you find yourself falling into the same traps? Do you reenact certain behaviors you have not only been avoiding but fighting against for so many years of your life? This isn't to shame you as you look backward at where you might have made some mistakes; it's to provide an adequate inventory of where you are susceptible to those traps. You are not alone.

It's not just parenting and calendars that leave me feeling as if I can't get my life together. There are more personal reasons as well.

I've been in counseling off and on for about a decade. I was hesitant about counseling at first, because I grew up believing that only the worst of the worst ended up in counseling. And in my very naive and judgmental mind, there were plenty of people worse off than me. My situation wasn't *that* tragic. I wasn't struggling *that* badly. I quickly learned that counseling can serve many different purposes. I know now that I need counseling when things are going well and when things are going poorly in my life. I need it when I think I have it all together *and* when everything seems to be falling apart.[v]

In a recent counseling session, I asked, "Will I ever stop bringing this up in here?" I had—once again—spent a considerable amount of time discussing a painful memory from more than twenty-five years ago. I bring this particular hurt up a lot. Sometimes I wonder if my counselor is rolling his eyes internally and questioning if I'll ever move on.

---

v. I'm a huge advocate for Christian counseling.

When I was nineteen years old, my dad made some choices that weren't the best for him or our family. No matter what is plaguing me on any particular day in the present, this moment of hurt from the past resurfaces, even after all these years.

I forgave my dad years ago. He is kind, funny, the life of the party, and he loves Jesus deeply. And yet it's still true that one of his greatest mistakes has caused one of my greatest wounds. We have a phenomenal relationship, and these past actions never define my dad or interfere with how I see him at all. Good gracious, my own life choices have certainly impacted people who love me! Every single one of us screws up so badly that we affect those around us in ways we hate.[vi] I understand this truth in my head, yet my heart, soul, and sometimes even my body keep returning to that moment in my life that has so greatly marked me. The pain is still so deep, and I can close my eyes and picture that day more clearly than any other day in my entire life.

As I take a close look at my reality today, I see so many parts of my life that, on my best days, I feel like I'm managing or, on my worst days, I feel are suffocating me. I try to take care of my body, and then I get stressed and turn back to old habits. I desire to think the best of my husband, and then he runs late coming home from work, and I jump to all the worst-case scenarios. I beg Jesus to give me patience with my kids, and then after one cup of spilled milk, we're all crying. My friend pours her heart out to me, and I tell her I'll pray for her, but then I forget entirely until I run into her at church the following week.

---

vi. I'm confident my children could write an entire trilogy of how my mistakes hurt them. Then my parents could write the prequel detailing how my mistakes hurt them. This isn't about my dad's mistakes. We all make them. This is just one wound that has deeply hurt me.

I hate this about myself, and yet here I am, sharing all my dirty laundry. I'm convinced that most of us wonder if we'll ever be able to get it together. The reality is we are humans who sin. We are frustrated because our life stage isn't accommodating our desires and wants. We continue to mess up. We've consistently overcommitted ourselves. Other people hurt us with their faults.

It is not the news you want to hear, but I do think it's the news you already know.

We're trying to "get it together" in areas we have no control over. We keep trying, but we'll never move the needle to a better future, because it has nothing to do with us or anything we can do.

We're trying to "get it together" in areas we have no control over. We keep trying, but we'll never move the needle to a better future, because it has nothing to do with us or anything we can do.

We don't have to always give in to what the world, our families, or our own self declares is the way things are "supposed" to be. Trying to live up to immeasurable standards that have been set for us by fellow sinners is never a great plan. It keeps us all running in place with nowhere to go.

Yet God desires goodness and joy for us. He has more available for us than we could ever begin to imagine, no matter what our current realities feel like. God, Jesus, and the Spirit went to great lengths to offer you and me the *best* good news ever. This promise is the only standard I want to live by.

Before we journey together through these pages, I want to set the groundwork for a few things. First off—gosh! I wish we were together! I wish we were sitting in my living room with a fire in the fireplace, my two awesome dogs at our feet, while my husband cooks for us, and we could talk through all of this in person.[vii] On a more serious note, I want you to know that the words you will read on these pages are words *I* needed. They are the words I have said to myself and the words that I'm still repeating to myself.

Different seasons in our lives bring about different hurdles for each of us. I truly believe that we often feel so frazzled because we aren't looking at our lives through the correct lens. We need a new perspective. When we have the right response to our current realities, we can get it together no matter what is happening in our lives.

> **When we have the right response to our current realities, we can get it together no matter what is happening in our lives.**

For some of us, there isn't a moment of hurt that keeps creeping back into our lives like the one I shared about my dad. Some of us are in a very present hurt that we can't seem to get away from. Some of us have small habits that we need to address or expectations that we've placed on ourselves or that others have put on us that we need to reevaluate and maybe even eliminate.

We are going to look at six areas of our lives that affect our perception of God's love. We're also going to dig deep into God's Word to see what it says about why we feel like we are not enough and how God feels about us in the midst of it all. I can't tell you exactly how "together" needs to look in your specific circumstance right at this moment. But I *can* share what I've learned in my own life about getting it together.

---

vii. You need to know that I love my dogs, I love a fire in the fireplace, and I love when Aaron cooks—so I'm welcoming you into my best day ever!

Friend, you are loved more than you could ever imagine. Your past and present do not have to define your future, and you can have peace—even if that life looks different from what you imagined. No matter what your current reality is, you *can* get it together.

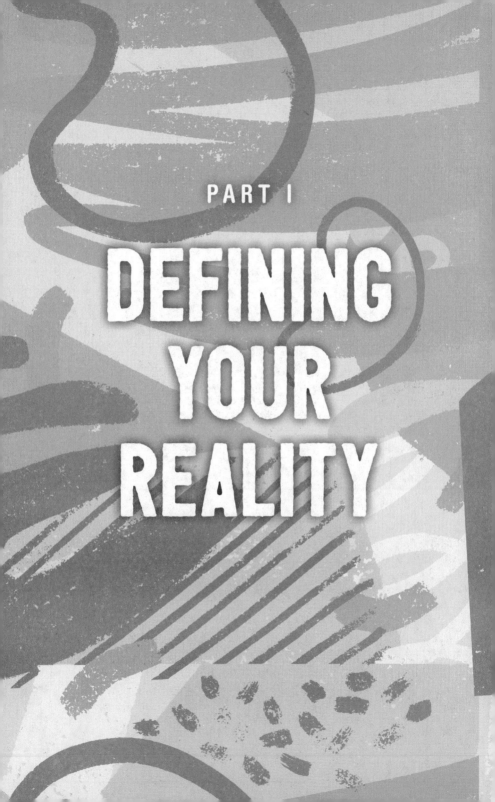

PART I

DEFINING YOUR REALITY

CHAPTER 1

UNICORNS AREN'T REALITY

Do you ever feel like you are holding on to life by a single fraying thread? Or like you might be chasing the wrong things in life? If you are a Christian, your main pursuit in life is to look, act, talk, and be more like Christ. That's what we should be chasing. But the world tells us to go after other things, so we become unsure or unclear about what to chase.

The idea of getting it together is such a mystery, but we all know it's something we want. To say I understand would be the understatement of the year. Some days I think getting it together means that I'm awake before the sun is up, spending time with God before I even leave my bedroom. It means I would shower *and* wash my hair *and* dry my hair, and then have spoken words of affirmation to everyone in my house before they all leave for school and work by 7:30 A.M. Of course, I would also value my body for all the right reasons and confidently say no to the third request for cookies for the high school bake sale. I feel like getting it together means trusting my husband's love, allowing myself to have emotions that truly reflect what's going on, and believing the best about people.

Some days I think, *If only I could be* that *girl, then I'd really have it together!*

I'm betting most of us are bringing so much to the table when it comes to considering what it means to get it together. We have past hurts, current hurts, responsibilities with our family and friends, and expectations from the church of what a "good" Christian looks like. We have failed dreams and overcommitted schedules. We have roommates, spouses, and kids who bring out the worst in us. We lay our heads down on our pillows to sleep and wonder how life got to be this way.

But what does it mean to get it together, and who decides this definition in your life and mine? *Merriam-Webster* defines *together* as:

- Appropriately prepared
- Organized
- Balanced

How many of those are you checking off? For me, it depends on the day, and often the hour, as to how together I feel—as Mr. Webster defines it. But "appropriately prepared" in my role as a podcaster and author is very different from being "appropriately prepared" as a mother and a wife. "Balance" for a college sophomore requires different priorities than it does for an empty nester. Life seasons and circumstances will change this definition for all of us. So how can we *all* get it together?

OUR DIFFERENT REALITIES

My company has an office location for those who don't work from home. Whenever my husband visits, he declares that there's no way he could *ever* work in my office space. There are books stacked on the floor all around the room. The desk has papers all over it. There's a sweatshirt in the corner and a jacket on the chair. To him, it's a disaster, but to me, it's perfection.

I know why each piece of paper is important and the categories of the different stacks of books, and if you aren't prepared for a chilly office with not one but *two* jackets, then who even are you? This is my idea of getting it together at work—being prepared with everything I need around me. My husband's idea of getting it together at work, on the other hand, would mean a spotless floor, a pristine desk, and a perfectly arranged shelf—being prepared with everything in its proper place. I find this quite boring, and I don't even know how he works with all that empty desk space staring at him. But, whatever. To each their own.

I've always wanted to be my best. And yet I have spent way too many hours trying to copy someone else's aspirations to feel like I'm doing it "right." When my kids were little, I worried about them making friends at school, and now I worry about which friends they are choosing to hang out with. I used to worry about us all getting to church with our shoes on, and now I worry about my kids even wanting to go to church. The definition of getting it together keeps shifting.

While my expectations for doing life with others is constantly changing, my personal needs can fluctuate as well. When it comes to taking care of my body, I wonder how everyone on Instagram makes it look so easy. Do they wake up every morning and choose to drink water all day? Somehow they get to the gym five times a week and still have a job and family and friends. I can't figure it out. No carbs? No sugar? No dairy? No fun! It's hard to find what makes me *feel* good and doesn't just push me toward wanting to look good. My body insecurities keep creeping up while I'm just trying to be healthy!

Of course, not all my personal goals resonate with you. We're all so different. My life is my life, and your life is yours. The goal isn't to make your life look like mine or vice versa. God has put us all in different places, with different relationships, different duties, different bodies, and different dreams.

If you are a college student, your time and capacity are very different from the mom with four young kids at home. Your ability to get more done at night looks different. For those of you in a season of retirement, your capacity to invest in your local church looks completely different than that of a woman who is working two jobs to support her family.

You will have unique expectations depending on what season you are in. But here's the exciting part: our individual realities are so different, and yet we can all redefine getting it together no matter what our current reality is.

OUR DIFFERENT CHOICES

It's important to address that sometimes we don't feel like we are on our A game because we have made different choices in our lives than those around us. We either look around and begin to doubt our decisions or we see those around us pointing out our different path, making us feel insecure. When we assume there is a one-size-fits-all blueprint for everything, it often leaves us feeling as if we aren't living up to some unattainable status quo.

Our individual realities are so different, and yet we can all redefine getting it together no matter what our current reality is.

Sometimes I struggle with the smallest of decisions. Seriously. I can hardly choose what to wear without texting five girlfriends about it, asking them to pick their favorite look, and then wearing whichever outfit gets the most votes. I constantly wonder if I should have made a different decision. It's a truly miserable way to live.

So when someone tells me that I can make my own choice, I feel empowered and intimidated all at the same time. And I don't think I'm alone. The number of decisions we make in our lifetime about things that don't have a right or wrong answer is overwhelming. If faced with the temptation to steal a purse from Target or possibly stab my neighbor, I know what to do. Those are moral issues that the Bible is very clear on. There's no gray area. Don't steal and don't stab. Easy as that.

But what about all the other decisions we spend our lives making? *What should I eat? Should I save or spend this paycheck? Should I sign up for PTA president, homeroom parent, or neither? Should I go to that football party at the university or stay home and study?* We make choices every day that don't affect the ultimate destiny of our lives. Hundreds and hundreds of small decisions. We also make big decisions that can change our lives—but there's no verse or chapter in the Bible to tell us what to do with these daily decisions.

As a mom to four kids, I'm making decisions for myself and others all the time. And over the years, I have been inundated with all the ways I *should* be parenting. Everyone has an opinion about what makes a good parent. And yet I often feel like the standard for "good" mom and dad is confusing and the target is always moving. And who is in charge of creating that standard anyway?[i]

---

i. I think it's actually *us*. We look around and create a standard that doesn't make sense based on culture and church norms.

As our kids have gotten older and are now in a season of making more of their own decisions, our parenting journey has shifted from being decision-makers to decision-helpers. They want to make their own choices about life—and they need to start learning how to do that while still in our house. I've had to push aside how the culture and/or the church tells me it's supposed to go:

- One son took a gap year instead of going to college right out of high school.
- Our kids are not expected to get married and have a family unless they feel called to do so.
- My kids' choice of music has been less important to me than I thought it would.
- One son decided to stop playing football when outside voices told him he needed to.
- My daughter got her nose pierced after another mom told me, "If you have to sign a consent, they are too young!"

Those things likely seem big to some of you and very minor to others, but I have to shake off what others tell me is the right way to raise my kids. It hasn't been easy, but when I finally realized that getting it together as a mom meant I had a choice in the matter, I found so much freedom! Part of getting it together is being confident about our choices, even when they aren't what someone else would choose. But how do we build that confidence?

Part of getting it together is being confident about our choices, even when they aren't what someone else would choose.

OUR DIFFERENT DECISIONS

I heard a sermon once that showed believers how to make a wise decision.[1] The preacher laid out four steps to decision-making.

1. **IS IT A SIN?** Go to the Bible and see if what you want to do is a sin. Stealing from Target is a sin. But a husband and wife choosing to not have children or a young man deciding to take an unpaid internship are not sins.
2. **ASK OTHER BELIEVERS.** Involve wise people in this decision-making time. Your community knows you best, so let them speak into these moments. Deciding what university you should attend, whether to have more kids, or whether to buy a house as a single woman are all great questions—which involve big decisions—so let your community love you well by walking with you as you decide.
3. **DO WHAT YOU WANT.** Make that decision. Choose! You looked through the Bible. You asked your people. Now decide!
4. **TRUST GOD WITH THE RESULTS.** Wise decisions don't always lead to the most desirable outcomes. Just think about Jesus. He made all perfectly wise decisions, and He ended up beaten, mocked, and crucified. Trust God with whatever comes after your wise decision.

You, my friend, have so much agency over your choices in life. You are fully capable of making decisions! I often tell myself: *Jamie, you are smart, wise, a follower of Jesus with the Spirit of God dwelling in you; you can make a decision that honors yourself, your family, and God.*

Letting someone else set your priorities for your life is a sure way to feel like a failure each day. We will always fail to meet the standards of others. However, if we take responsibility for our own journeys while trusting that ultimate control lies with God, we can hold our heads high as we move through our lives.

Letting someone else set your priorities for your life is a sure way to feel like a failure each day.

Take reading our Bibles, for example. I don't think anyone pursuing a relationship with Jesus would say that reading the Bible isn't important. Yet we often try to set unrealistic standards for ourselves for Bible reading, and when we don't meet them, we feel like a failure. When I was in high school, reading my Bible looked different from when I was in college. As a single woman, my Bible reading looked different from when I got married. Being a mom to toddlers and spending time with Jesus and His Word looked a million times different than it does now as a mom to teenagers with a full-time job.

My standard and your standard of getting it together will be completely different. This doesn't negate good things we should be doing, or even right and moral things. We often take good and right things and try to force everyone into the same box. Then, when we don't fit that standard, we declare ourselves failures. We tell ourselves to get it together every morning when our Bible reading time looks different from what we perceive is the right way to do this.

It's why you, my friend, need to make good decisions about what your life needs at this moment. This isn't a way to get out of doing what we need to do, fulfilling our commitments, or dealing with our past traumas. But it is a way to take an inventory of and set standards for your life based on your capacity, schedule, and needs for success and growth. Then, whether you read your Bible at 5 A.M. or 1:15 P.M., you know your priorities for your season of life.

IT'S ABOUT YOUR DEFINITION

We have already established two important truths: we all have different realities, and we need to confidently make our own choices. Both of those truths help us get to our shared definition of getting it together: having the right responses to our current circumstances.

"Reality is a friend of intimacy with God. Denial is an enemy," Alicia Britt Chole shared recently at a retreat I attended. It's so true. No two people are living the same story every day, and there are real truths about each of our lives that impact the way we feel about ourselves. This feeling of discontentment rises inside of us when we are not responding to the current moment in the right way. And when we choose to overlook the realities of our circumstances—good and bad—we are refusing to respond to our lives from an overflow of God's love for us. The way we respond to our reality is an indicator of our intimacy and relationship with God.

In 2009, our family hosted a child from Haiti on a medical visa. This little girl was born with spina bifida and needed a crucial surgery to help her survive and thrive in her home country. I flew to Florida to meet a missionary friend who lives in Haiti as she flew to the States with this sweet child. In the airport, I was united with a scared and anxious three-year-old, who immediately clung to me as if she knew I

The way we respond to our reality is an indicator of our intimacy and relationship with God.

was her only hope. We created a bond that to this day still brings me to tears.

This little girl lived with our family for nine weeks, and she and I spent a lot of time in the hospital together as she endured surgery and recovery. I fell in love with her and never underestimated the trust her parents put in our family. We loved her as our own, always knowing she wasn't.

Those nine weeks were one of our family's hardest seasons. She and I cried many tears and spent many lonely nights in hospital rooms where she was scared and I was missing my kids and husband. My realities were changed overnight, and most of my frustrations were birthed from not allowing myself the grace to not be able to do it all—which meant a messy house, my absence from the dinner table, and my reliance on so many friends. This was a hard reality for me.

When your circumstances change overnight like ours did, you will never feel put together if you keep the standard the same as before. Previous to hosting this medically fragile child, I had a great schedule with my boys, and now I had multiple doctor visits and numerous overnight hospital stays in my schedule. My new reality needed a new perspective, and with that new perspective I needed the grace and mercy of Jesus to help me readjust my expectations of myself.

Together, we're going to walk through these different areas of life. We're going to get to a point where we can confidently say that just because something is hard doesn't mean it's bad. You will be able to look at all areas of your life and see what needs readjusting, what needs more counseling, what needs to be laid down, and what needs to be picked up.

The best resource we have to determine if we are demonstrating the right response to our realities is to examine how Jesus responded to people. Did we see Jesus encounter sick people and ask them to confront their past wounds before He healed them? Did we see Jesus ask women to clean their homes before He would enter? Did we see Him encourage His disciples to get a good education before they could follow Him?

The answer is no. The way Jesus responded to the people around Him should be our standard of response to *ourselves*. Compassion. Grace. Mercy. Acknowledging the difficult times and seasons.

Our measure of what our lives should be like—the measure of getting it together—must acknowledge our present state. When a mother of two children has just lost her husband from cancer, we look at her reality and tell her that she doesn't need to do anything but grieve, rest, and take care of her kids. From her perspective, she might feel embarrassed about her messy house when people bring food over. She might tell herself that a "good" mom would have already cleaned up the dishes from last night's dinner before someone showed up with dinner for today. When our circumstances shift, we have trouble shifting our perception of what getting it together means and showing ourselves grace in the process.

> **When our circumstances shift, we have trouble shifting our perception of what getting it together means and showing ourselves grace in the process.**

CHAPTER 2

EVERYTHING IS BROKEN

Have you ever dived into your own lineage? A few Christmases ago, my mom gave me and my brother an amazing gift.[i] I opened the box and was both confused and intrigued to find a gigantic three-ring binder. As I pulled out the binder and opened it up, I realized it was my own history in my hands. My mom had given me my very own family tree!

The binder contained pictures, birth and death certificates, and newspaper clippings about my grandparents and their parents. But the best part is that, because of some work my grandmother started before she passed away, my mom could trace our family trees back several hundred years. Somebody in my family was even on the *Mayflower*. How cool is that? And like many Americans, I could see that my family originated from all over the world. I glanced over it quickly, smiled big, and thanked my mom. I knew this was a treasure.

---

i. I know this gift is cool if you are middle-aged and not a teenager or a young adult. If she had given my teens this gift, they would have declared it the worst Christmas ever! But I'm in my forties, so this gift was amazing.

This idea of being born into something can feel tricky to many of us. Three of my children joined our family through adoption, so their bloodline has nothing to do with their status as an Ivey. They didn't start out as an Ivey, and they don't have any of the same DNA as me or my husband, and yet their legal status is "Ivey." When their adoptions were complete, they were each declared an Ivey, their life trajectories changed, and they received deep roots on our family tree.

Recently, I was thinking about that binder, and I pulled it down from the top of my closet and dove in. I read the names of generations in the past and imagined what they had endured for me to be here today. I wondered if any of them had loved Jesus. I wondered if any of them had owned slaves. I wondered if any of them had watched loved ones lose their lives.[ii]

One thing I thought about as I looked through pages and pages of lives I'll never know or understand is that although their struggles were different in some ways from mine today, they also probably dealt with the same emotions I feel.

They felt lonely.
They felt insecure.
They felt less-than.

I'm sure some of them also felt they could never get it together.

Although they lived in different eras and places, they were still human. And since the very beginning of time, we humans have suffered in all sorts of ways. If we go all the way back to the very beginning of time when God created humans, we can gain some insight into why our lives sometimes feel messy and so out of control.

---

ii. My mom's side has family members who walked the Trail of Tears in the 1800s.

GARDENS

Let me set the scene for you way back when God set the world into motion (see Genesis 2). God created all things, yet there was no one to cultivate the ground, so He formed the man from the ground's soil and breathed the breath of life into his nostrils. The man was now living! The Lord then placed the man inside the orchard in Eden to care for it and maintain it. Inside this orchard were all kinds of trees that were pleasing to look at and good for food. Two of those trees are described for us in Scripture. There was the Tree of Life and the Tree of Knowledge of Good and Evil—both located in the center of the orchard.

God then told the man that he could eat freely from any tree in the garden *except* the Tree of Knowledge of Good and Evil. He told the man that if he ate from it, he would surely die. One rule—that's it. Eat whatever you want. Roam wherever you want. Live it up. Just follow one rule. God then made Adam a helper suitable for him, and his new bride, Eve, was perfectly content in the garden.

This is where the whole thing starts to unravel and go downhill. Temptation entered the garden as a serpent who convinced Eve that God was holding out on her and that He didn't truly have the best intentions for her. Oh, there it is—the lie we so often believe about God. He doesn't truly love us. He is holding out on us. There must be more to this life than all I have been given and promised.

Eve and Adam ate from the Tree of Knowledge of Good and Evil, and from that moment, nothing has ever been the same. Everything broke. Our first parents brought sin into this world, and it's been running in our blood ever since.

I often wonder if Eve remembered and thought about that

moment in the garden for the rest of her life. I have no clue, and the Bible doesn't give a ton of details on her life after the garden. But I do know that she had one rule to follow and one job to do, and she failed at it. I have felt like Eve a million times in my lifetime.

The message here is not "It's just what we do, so keep dropping those balls." We have hope. The very first humans dropped the *only* ball they had to deal with. The only one! Adam and Eve had it all together, until they didn't. We can see so much of ourselves in them. And the good news is that from Genesis 3 through the rest of the Bible, God shows us how He will make it all right again. Their story doesn't end with failure, and neither does yours!

> Therefore, just as sin came into the world through one man, and death through sin, . . . so death spread to all men because all sinned.
>
> ROMANS 5:12

All those centuries ago, everything changed for humanity. I know it can seem complex and super unfair that we are punished for something we had no choice in. I get it. But God, in His kindness, never intended to leave us stuck in our sin. He planned to send His Son to redeem that sinful stain on us all.

> But the free gift is not like the trespass. For if many died through one man's trespass, much more have the grace of God and the free gift by the grace of that one man Jesus Christ abounded for many. . . . For if, because of one man's trespass, death reigned through that one man, much more will those who receive the abundance of grace and the free gift of righteousness reign in life through the one man Jesus Christ. Therefore, as one trespass led

to condemnation for all men, so one act of righteousness leads to justification and life for all men.

ROMANS 5:15, 17–18

As Angie Smith says, "The root reason for why sin is *in* us is because our first parents decided not to trust God. They fell. And we became their fallen children."[1] We fail time and time again because we don't believe that God loves us. We are sinners in need of a Savior, and we will continue to fail until the day we see Jesus. As His followers, we should desire to look more and more like Him, which means we seek to live in such a way that sin doesn't reign in our bodies trying to make us obey its passions (Romans 6:12).

I've been following Jesus for a little over two decades. I have spent years trying to look more like Him and realizing I will never fully succeed while I'm here on this earth. Sin is what keeps me from that desire. I truly want to do what is right in the sight of God, and yet I also live in a world that is screaming at me to do whatever I want. It's the burden we all carry every day.

I recently got into a fight with my husband—again. Basically, the same fight we have been in a million and one times before. I got my feelings hurt. His pride was smashed. We said mean things. I felt afraid, and he felt demeaned. It's the worst dance we do together. We spew hateful words and retreat into ourselves in silence. Every time it happens, I hate it. We apologized after a few hours and began to find that dance back to each other. As a follower of Jesus and wife for twenty-some-odd years, I find this sin to be disgusting. I don't want to continue this way, and while I am so much further along than I was ten years ago, one year ago, and even one day ago, I still have so far to go.

My mean words to my husband are a small example of how sin

keeps creeping into my life. It can feel defeating to be back in the place you don't want to be.

You might be thinking to yourself, "Jamie, I wish my biggest failure was as tame as this example." You might find yourself relating more to Eve in your day-to-day moments of doing exactly what God asked you not to do. Your sinful patterns and habits have stayed for too long, yet you keep coddling them. Me too.

You are not alone.

A LINEAGE OF FAILURE

There was a time in my life years ago when I used to sign up to take meals to people after they had a baby. It's very much the kind, Christian, southern thing to do. You get the meal calendar email, and your job is twofold: pick a date, then show up with food. It's really not that hard.

Except for me. For some of us, this is the hardest thing we will do in a day. But I did what a good friend would do and signed up for the meal. I probably even put it on my calendar because I'm very dedicated to living by my calendar. The selected day rolled around, and I did nothing. In fact, the meal never entered my mind until about 5:30 P.M. when I received a text from my hungry friend because she was curious about what time I'd be dropping off dinner for her and her family of five. She wanted to plan bath time around it, so she was just checking in.

I remember reading her text as I stood in my kitchen, where I'd been trying to figure out what I would feed my own children. My husband, Aaron, was out of town, and he is the main chef in our home. But I was in charge that night, and it was that time of day when everyone is grouchy and just needs to eat before the whole house gets burned down. I looked at that text and said, "Jamie, you couldn't even do the *one thing* you were supposed to do today." Fail. I had failed. I had failed my friend. And her family of five.

The story of forgetting my friend's meal seems minor compared to other things we drop the ball on in our lives. I get it. I've failed to pick the kids up from school before. I've missed meeting up with a friend who needed to process the hardship in her life. But more than mistakes, I've willingly continued to indulge in sinful patterns and habits I'd want no one to know about. I've eaten to comfort my emotions, drank too much to mask any pain I'm feeling, neglected caring for my body, spent money that wasn't available, treated my kids poorly, yelled at my husband, felt contempt toward a coworker, intentionally left someone out—and the list goes on and on.

When we step back and remember that our flesh is always out to gratify its own desires, it puts a different spin on what getting it together means. It reminds us that our feelings of failing again, letting down those we love, or doing what we don't want to do come from a place so deep inside us. Sin is here to stay. That doesn't mean we are owned by sin or defeated by it, but it does mean we are sinners (Romans 6:6, 11). It means that we need to be fully aware of our weaknesses and downfalls to fight and kill sin. Everything is broken, and because of that, we feel the aftershocks of that day long ago in Genesis 3 when Adam and Eve chose not to believe that God truly loved them.

> Everything is broken, and because of that, we feel the aftershocks of that day long ago in Genesis 3 when Adam and Eve chose not to believe that God truly loved them.

For some of us, this idea of everything starting out broken before you even get a chance to do it right is defeating. For others, it brings a big sigh of relief. No matter what camp you find yourself in, there is truth here that helps us move forward on the path to getting it together. These are the truths we're building on:

- God created the world, and it was good.
- God gave Adam and Eve one rule to follow.
- Adam and Eve chose not to trust God, and because of that, sin entered the world and is still here today.
- You and I are still living in a world that includes sin, and it affects everything in our lives.

God never intended to leave His people without hope. This is what the Bible calls *good news*. "God loved his children too much to let the story end there. Even though he knew he would suffer, God had a plan—a magnificent dream. One day, he would get his children back. One day, he would make their world their perfect home again. And one day, he would wipe away every tear from their eyes."[iii]

I'm here to tell you that it's not just the *good news*, it's the *best news*!

Sin will always result in spiritual death (separation from God), but there is a gift from God, and it is eternal life in Jesus (Romans 6:23). Christ was sent into the world to save God's people from eternal separation from Him. This is the greatest hope we have! Trusting in Jesus changes everything in your life. It brings peace, hope, and joy where only despair, anxiety, and hopelessness existed. Sure, these feelings still exist in us, but they don't rule us anymore. They can't. Jesus defeated them all.

---

iii. This is an excerpt from *The Jesus Storybook Bible* by Sally Lloyd-Jones. If you haven't read it, go order it now. It says it's for children, but it's really for all of us!

OUR ONLY HOPE

One of the greatest mysteries in all of creation is Jesus. Why would a perfect, holy God die for the same people who chose not to trust Him? The same people who couldn't follow the one rule set before them. The ones who chose their own desires over the perfection offered by God.

Those people, Adam and Eve—they are us. You and me. Their disobedience is our disobedience, and we all need redemption and freedom. Gosh, do I know this sounds and often feels unfair. Yet Jesus was always going to take care of all of us, even in the midst of this disobedience.

Romans 5 expands on the glorious truth that God loved us when we were unlovable. Because of His love for us and Jesus' sacrifice for us, we are reconciled to God. When sin separated humanity from God in the garden, Jesus' death on the cross reconciled us to Him.

> Christ arrives right on time to make this happen. He didn't, and doesn't, wait for us to get ready. He presented himself for this sacrificial death when we were far too weak and rebellious to do anything to get ourselves ready. And even if we hadn't been so weak, we wouldn't have known what to do anyway. We can understand someone dying for a person worth dying for, and we can understand how someone good and noble could inspire us to selfless sacrifice. But God put his love on the line for us by offering his Son in sacrificial death while we were of no use whatever to him.
>
> ROMANS 5:6–8 MSG

We did nothing to deserve this sacrifice, yet Jesus gave Himself up to death for us anyway. There was no grudge held against humanity. There wasn't a time when we were asked to get ourselves right before God. God sent Jesus despite our sin. It couldn't keep Jesus off the cross. It sent Him there.

> Now that we are set right with God by means of this sacrificial death, the consummate blood sacrifice, there is no longer a question of being at odds with God in any way. If, when we were at our worst, we were put on friendly terms with God by the sacrificial death of his Son, now that we're at our best, just think of how our lives will expand and deepen by means of his resurrection life! Now that we have actually received this amazing friendship with God, we are no longer content to simply say it in plodding prose. We sing and shout our praises to God through Jesus, the Messiah!
>
> ROMANS 5:9–11 MSG

Friends, we are on good terms with God because of Jesus and Jesus alone. We aren't on good terms because we're good people, because we make good choices, or because we're pros at getting it together. Our *only* hope is Jesus. As we journey through life and often feel discouraged about our failures and screwups, let us all remember the lengths that God went to bring us back to Him—to make us His children.

When you and I really and truly understand that we did not deserve God's grace and love, it changes how we live—the way we think. We sing a song at church that says, "Turn my eyes to see You, Jesus, in all Your glory. Tune my heart to sing in wonder of how You love me. Center my life on Your name."[2] The truth of God redeeming our brokenness that has been a part of humanity since the beginning of time causes me to desire to center my entire life on Him. I pray it does for you too.

So, if everything in this world is broken, what do we do to move forward?

CHAPTER 3

P.O.N.D.E.R.

If getting it together is having the right responses to your current reality, then we need to talk about all the different aspects of your daily life. I believe this is what makes tackling the idea of getting it together so difficult. The truth is that every one of us reading these words has vastly different circumstances in our current reality.[i]

You might be in your twenties trying to figure out your next steps in life, or in your forties also trying to figure out your next steps in life—but those "next steps" would be so different! We can see this just looking around us. Think about your friends. Think about the vast number of different circumstances represented in just that group. No two of your friends are living with the exact same histories, dreams, personalities, abilities, and so on. Every single one of us brings a different reality to the table when figuring out how to get it together. This means we need to get specific. We must figure out what getting it together means for *you* and *your* current reality. Remember, getting it together is having the right response to

---

i. And let's be honest, your circumstances could change from day to day! I get it!

your current reality, so step one is to consider—or PONDER—your current reality thoughtfully. Your current circumstances are made up of six areas.

PONDER—THE SIX AREAS OF YOUR REALITY

- **P**ast and present hurts—*I am hurting from . . .*
- **O**bligations—*I said that I would . . .*
- **N**eeds—*I need _____ for my health*
- **D**esires—*I want to do/be . . .*
- **E**xpectations—*I should . . .*
- **R**esponsibilities—*I have to . . .*

Our realities are so complex because we are complex. As you read this list, some areas probably jumped out at you more than others. But each is important to consider. We will focus here on your current reality as it stands today. As you enter new life stages and new circumstances and complexities arise, your reality will change, and you will have a new current reality to ponder. You likely picked up this book because one or more of these areas is oversized in your current reality and is affecting the others. We'll dive deeper into each area to ponder in future chapters, but here's a quick description of the six reality areas:

Past and present hurts—*I am hurting from . . .*

Like me, you might have a past hurt, or you might be in the midst of some very present hurts. Your life is not going as you expected, you are in the midst of suffering, or you feel as though you might not make it through the day. Your heart is hurt. Your soul

26

is hurt. Of course, you don't feel as though you can get it together. How could you?

If this is you, pause now and breathe deeply. Know that on this journey I will never ask you to put on your big girl panties and simply get over it. We're often tempted to gloss over our pain and put on our happy Christian face during hardships. You wouldn't ask a friend with a broken arm to act like nothing is wrong, and we're not going to do that with your hurting heart either.

Obligations—*I said that I would . . .*

Some of you have overextended yourselves. You've said yes to too many things, and now you have too many obligations. Everyone assumes you can do it because you always do. They ask *you* because they know you'll say yes. You have a smile on your face, but late at night, you struggle with anxiety over all the things you didn't get done. You tell everyone that you are fine, but your home is falling apart, and the things that need to be done in your own life aren't happening.

Needs—*I need _____ for my health*

Some of us aren't taking good care of ourselves. We forget we have our own needs. We expend our energy on everyone around us, yet here we are again, getting the doctor's report that something needs to change for our own health and well-being. It's not about looking good; it's about ensuring our bodies are getting the best of us so we can give the best. And we must remember that our bodies include our minds and our souls—they are hard to separate!

Desires—*I want to do/be . . .*

Maybe you have big dreams. You want to travel or to have a savings account that actually has money in it. You desire to be generous with your money, but you find yourself aimlessly scrolling Instagram at night and purchasing things you think you need. You dream of making that big career move but struggle to do the hard work you know it will require. Or maybe it's tennis lessons, finishing your book, or memorizing the entire book of Romans. But do you have room in your reality for these dreams? Are you setting goals and working toward them? Are they things you should really want, or are they getting between you and God? You have things you desire, but often you get in the way of these things.

Expectations—*I should* . . .

Our realities fill up with unrealistic expectations—from ourselves and others—and those expectations can be suffocating for us. We find ourselves consumed with what we think we *should* be doing or what *others* tell us we should be doing. We can become consumed with expecting ourselves to be further ahead in life than we actually are. Is your reality full of what you think you should or ought to be doing? Are you living in a world of *should*?

Responsibilities—*I have to* . . .

And lastly, there are responsibilities—things in life we have to deal with. These vary greatly from person to person because they're largely based on our roles and relationships. Spouses and parents have some clear jobs they have to complete for their families. Being a citizen of a certain country, owning a car, having a roommate, being a student, or maintaining employment all come with responsibilities.

These six areas make up your personal, current existence. When life feels chaotic, it's usually because the circumstances in one or more of these areas are outsized and overwhelming. You'll likely never have a perfect balance among all categories. In different seasons of life, certain areas will take more of your time and attention than others. In specific life circumstances, your focus might be consumed by a single area because it's full of tension and struggles.

When I first began working full-time, my tension with my areas of responsibilities and obligations was high. I felt torn and like someone was always getting the worst of me. As I removed some obligations (things I said yes to) and external expectations (things I thought I should be doing) from my plate, my reality balanced out. The older I get, the more my health needs are taking priority. I haven't had to deal with any major health issues, but I'm now managing all the appointments I need to stay healthy in the back half of my life.

The areas of obligations, expectations, and responsibilities can sometimes be confusing for people. Let's explore these areas by using parenting as an example. I am responsible for my children in so many ways. If I don't take care of their basic needs, the state can remove them from my home. I not only need to feed them and clothe them but, because I'm a follower of Jesus, I have responsibilities to love them and care for them as well. Some expectations that I might put on myself, or allow others to put on me, would be to have well-behaved kids that get straight As and never lose their temper. We live in the South, so they should also say "yes ma'am" and "no ma'am" when addressing adults and always have a smile on their faces. Those expectations are sometimes unrealistic. Lastly, if I tell my kids that I will take them to the water park every Friday during the summer, that is an obligation that I created for myself. I gave them my yes, and now I need to follow through.

As I mentioned before, the first step in getting it together is to ponder your current reality. According to the dictionary, to ponder something is to think about it deeply before coming to a conclusion, which means you need a clear picture of what you're dealing with.

I'm going to ask you to complete a Reality Inventory. This list is not meant for you to see what you need to remove from your life and start crossing things out, although that might happen. This exercise is for you to take a personal assessment of your circumstances today. When we slow down and get things out of our heads and onto paper, our reality becomes clearer to us. So get it all out—the more, the better!

As you make your Reality Inventory, fight the negative feelings that may begin to surface. Your list of things in your life that feel hard might evoke or reinforce shame—don't let it! Your feelings might come from not having many things to fill in one category or too many in another. Remember, your current life stage affects these areas greatly! If you are in your twenties and don't have a history of breast cancer, you might not be stressed about scheduling your next mammogram as a need. If you are in your fifties and have an empty house, your responsibilities look different from a young woman in college.

Your current circumstances are uniquely yours and are personal to you. Look at your life closely and thoughtfully consider it. Take some time right now to pause in your reading and do this exercise. Find a pen so you can write down thoughts, or grab your journal if that's your thing. Maybe you need to do it digitally—that works too. The point is to see the six areas of your current reality in front of you.

WHERE YOUR REALITY NEEDS WORK

Begin your Reality Inventory in prayer. Ask God for help, whether that's bringing things to mind, calming your nerves, or giving you the courage to be honest. Tell Him that you trust Him and love Him, and ask Him to help you remember that He's right there in the room with you.

Under each category, list everything in your life that falls into that topic. Refer back to the description of the six areas if you need to, or use the "I" statements for each area to help you.

Past and present hurts—*I am hurting from . . .*

_____

_____

_____

_____

_____

Obligations—*I said that I would . . .*

_____

_____

_____

_____

_____

Needs—*I need_____ for my health*

_____

_____

Desires—*I want to do/be . . .*

Expectations—*I should . . .*

Responsibilities—*I have to . . .*

_____

_____

_____

_____

As we talk about suffering, pain, failure, and regret in future chapters, you will consider these six areas even more. Again, getting it together is having the right response to our current reality, so we need to have a clear picture of our current state. This exercise is intended for you to reference and reevaluate throughout your journey of getting it together. It's an important tool as we learn what the right response is and how to take our questions and feelings to Jesus—all while trying to look, act, live, and talk more like Him.

Again, getting it together is having the right response to our current reality, so we need to have a clear picture of our current state.

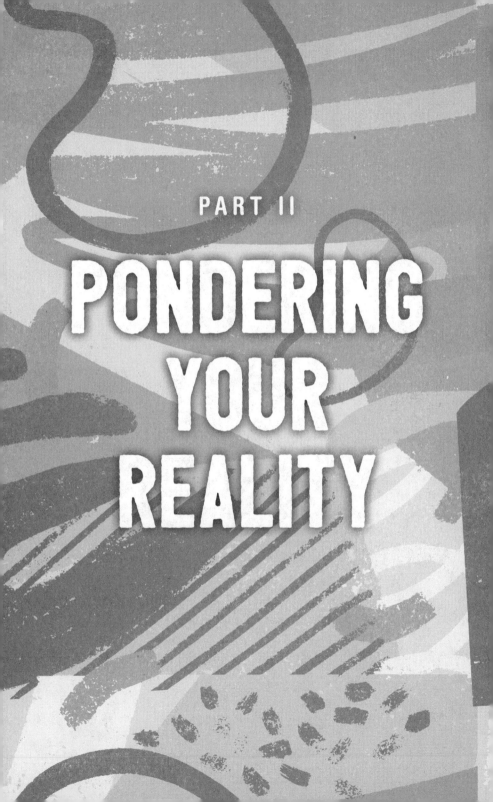

PART II

PONDERING YOUR REALITY

CHAPTER 4

BE KIND TO YOURSELF

PONDER YOUR PAST AND PRESENT HURTS

A few years ago, I sat face-to-face with my counselor, pouring out my fears about parenting, talking and crying at the same time. I had been parenting for seventeen years, and most days, I still felt as though I had no idea what I was doing. I listed all the ways I thought I had failed. Everything from conflicting thoughts on spanking to the lack of praying for their salvation to that one time we were vegetarians and I got mad at my child for eating the meat at school in the cafeteria. I'm sparing you so many other ridiculous and real ways I felt like a failure, but let me tell you, that cafeteria meat sauce nearly took me out. Failure mom moment for sure.

I expressed my fear that I had screwed up my kids. Would they ever know Jesus? Did they know I loved them? As I looked back on their younger years, I felt as though I had failed them. I told my therapist how hard it was for me to parent four kids under the age of six.

I shared about my exhaustion and how, with all the knowledge I have now on parenting kids from hard places, I would have done things differently. Aaron and I had learned so much over the past few years about trauma and mental health and parenting practices that we didn't know early on. I constantly felt like we had missed out on implementing them. That we were going to end up on the "bad parents" list. I shared all the ways I was confident my kids would hate me for a lifetime. I recounted all the things they would one day be processing with their own counselors about their mom.[i]

My counselor stopped my cycle of self-shame by asking me to perform a simple task. Pulling up an empty chair beside me, he told me to imagine someone in that chair—and not just any person, but me at age thirty-two. Age-thirty-two Jamie was parenting a six-year-old, two four-year-olds, and a two-year-old.[ii] Then he asked me to look at my thirty-two-year-old self and talk to her. "What do you want her to know?" he asked. "What do you want to say to her?"

As tears streamed down my face, I looked at this imaginary thirty-two-year-old version of myself in the empty chair next to me and tenderly told her, "You are doing the best you know, and I see you working so hard to love your people well. You are tired, and yet you are trying. You are worn out, and yet you are showing up. You feel ill-equipped, and quite frankly, you probably are. You are doing the best you know how."

He nodded and told me how kind I was to say that to her. He then asked if I truly believed what I said. I nodded. His next words have altered the way I look back on my life. He told me that when

---

i. I feel like as parents we should all give our kids free counseling for their twenty-fifth birthdays!
ii. I'm literally tired and weepy thinking about that time of my life.

I start to think about those years when my kids were little, and I want to beat myself up about mistakes I might have made, I should remember this version of myself—the thirty-two-year-old doing the best she knows how to love her people well—and extend kindness toward her.

OUR JOURNEY

It's so easy for us to look back on our past actions and criticize ourselves endlessly. Sure, there are certain things we need to be held accountable for and to acknowledge the pain we caused others or the missteps we took through our sinful actions. But there are also times we need to look back and realize we were immature, young, growing, and did not yet understand certain aspects of life, leading to bad choices. Maya Angelou is credited with saying, "Do the best you can until you know better. Then when you know better, do better." This quote brings me so much comfort when thinking about all the things I wish I could go back and do over.

Motherhood is like this for me. My younger self often felt like she was drowning in a body of water that she loved and wanted, yet it was often so much more than she could handle. When I look back on her with kindness, I can see the things I wish I would have done differently and, in the same breath, remind myself that she was doing the best she could. Today I don't dwell on how I could have been a better mom; I look and see that the hand of God was holding me up, even when I could feel water up to my neck.

Now in my midforties, I was driving with my daughter yesterday, and she told me, as confident as ever, that I was "getting old." I reminded her that I may be only halfway through my existence on this earth, and the first twenty years don't even count[iii]—which means I'm just getting started!

As I think about walking with Jesus for over two decades now, I'm confident of my growth in Him. It's been so evident. When I think about baby-Christian Jamie compared to Jamie today, I can see a ton of growth. We expect ourselves to have arrived at our full potential immediately, so when we have moments of frustration, sin, immaturity, or just plain stupidity, we beat ourselves up relentlessly over them.

As I have matured, I give myself more grace and get on my knees and beg for forgiveness more often. There's a sense of sanctification[iv] in my days. As I make mistakes in parenting, leadership, and friendships, I have an attitude that desires growth, whereas, in the past, there was more of a "what the actual heck is wrong with you, Jamie?!" attitude.

> We expect ourselves to have arrived at our full potential immediately, so when we have moments of frustration, sin, immaturity, or just plain stupidity, we beat ourselves up relentlessly over them.

First Corinthians 13:11 says, "When I was a child, I spoke like a child, I thought like a child, I reasoned like a child. When I became a man, I gave up childish ways." Paul was writing to the church in Corinth and reminding them how they should love each other. He described how the church should look and act, and this verse is right there at the tail end of all those words

---

iii. All of those years before we turn twenty are full of hormones and high school drama—I think we'd all agree we'd like to leave them behind!

iv. A big word for how God makes us look more and more like Jesus every day.

we use at weddings about what love is. Paul was showing us what growth looks like. A young child makes decisions that make sense for a young child. An adult (usually) makes decisions that make sense for an adult. A mature walking-with-Jesus adult should make decisions that reflect that walk and wisdom. Hopefully, you can look at your life and see the growth in your current choices.

Following Jesus year after year should produce good things in us. It doesn't make us perfect, but we should be able to look back and see growth in our lives. As Alicia Britt Chole says, "The decisions we make in difficult places today are greatly the product of decisions we made in the unseen places of yesterday."[1] As you note your growth and God's goodness, also note your journey to get here. It's not the beginning or the end of a journey that makes us who we are—it's everything along the way.

OUR MISTAKES

I've parented multiple sixteen-year-olds learning to drive.[v] I vividly remember teaching my oldest. Those days were so stressful and I hated it. I was an anxious mess—who then made *them* anxious! They made stupid mistakes that I declared were going to end both of our lives. I wondered how I could ever teach them all the things they needed to know to be safe. Fast-forward a few years, and today they are reliable drivers. They just needed some practice. Experience is the best teacher.

---

v. There's no trophy or medal for this, but there should be! Teaching a child to drive is one of my *least* favorite things to do in life. Our first three did an at-home learning program on our computer with our supervision, but our fourth and final driver is already enrolled in a class with a teacher who doesn't have our last name or live in our house. You get my drift. I am not teaching another kid to drive. I am done.

It's not the beginning or the end of a journey that makes us who we are— it's everything along the way.

It's like that with our Christian lives too. There's no way I can look back at my past self and compare that love for the Lord, that awareness of my sin, that talent, or that parenting to my current self. I have lived a lot of life since I became an adult. I've made a lot of mistakes. I've asked for a lot of forgiveness and forgiven others. In that time, my relationship with God has deepened, matured, and grown so beautifully intimate. And I'm so grateful, because life hasn't gotten any easier.

I've had thousands of conversations over the years, and the verdict is the same with everyone: life is just plain hard. There's no way around it. You can't go over, around, or under it; you must go through it. And though it often leaves us battered and bruised, we are somehow still standing. The stories of hurt that have been shared with me as a podcast host are often unbearable—seasons of loss, stories of injustices, and prolonged times of physical and emotional pain that my guests thought would take them out. Yet most of them tell me their stories through tears of remembrance, bearing the scars, somehow better on the other side of it.[vi]

The thing about being a follower of Jesus is that we experience the same difficulties in life as those who don't follow Him. Jesus never tells us that we will live an easy life. In fact, He says the exact opposite: "Take up [your] cross and follow me" (Matthew 16:24). The difference for us as believers is that amid all the hard stuff in life, we have something unbelievers don't: peace and comfort. The world

---

vi. "Better" isn't always what we imagine it would be.

says that it's unnatural to experience peace and comfort during trials. Jesus says, "Peace I leave with you; my peace I give you. I do not give to you as the world gives. Do not let your hearts be troubled and do not be afraid" (John 14:27 NIV). It's almost inexplicable, and unless you have experienced it, it sounds pretty unbelievable.

Some of you have experienced more pain in one lifetime than should be allowed for one person. Pain doesn't care who causes it; it still stings the same. Your past hurts could have been caused by decisions you had no say in, or you may be feeling the effects of your own choices. This pain can often leave scars on us, physically and emotionally. Beth Moore writes in her memoir, "For those of you that have lived past third grade, there's no real starting over from scratch. There's just starting over *scratched*, and if the hurts clawed deep enough, *scarred*."[2]

OUR SCARS

I have a rather sloppy scar on my lower abdomen from an emergency surgery when I was twenty-one. I followed Jesus as best I knew, having given Him all of my heart and soul eight months earlier, but I found myself pregnant and having emergency surgery to remove an ectopic pregnancy that had ruptured.[vii] That scar is big and ragged, because their main goal was to save my life and not my vanity. It's now a couple of decades after that surgery. At first, I despised that scar. It reminded me that even when I was following Jesus, I was making the very same mistakes I had been making before following Him. I was so embarrassed by the scar. It's not like anyone else could

---

vii. I tell this whole story in my book *If You Only Knew*.

see it, but when I saw it, I spoke harshly to myself and about myself. I wondered how a person who was following Jesus could make the same mistakes again. Wasn't I a new creation? Wasn't I a new person?

The kindness I have recently developed for the young girl I used to be is monumental. I see her with compassionate eyes, and I speak kindly about her. She was doing her best, stumbling to give Jesus everything He was asking of her. I keep thinking of this line from a novel I read years ago: "Because take it from me, a scar does not form on the dying. A scar means I survived."[3]

When I think back on my pregnancy before I was married, the trials I've had as a parent, or even the wounds of my childhood, I try to see myself as God sees me. Dr. Alison Cook says, "The goal is not to eradicate parts of your soul carrying anger, fear, sadness, envy, or shame, but to lead them with curiosity and compassion."[4] I lean into those emotions now. I get curious about where my emotions are coming from, and that curiosity always leads me toward having more compassion for myself. God sees me as His child whom He adores and loves forever. He sees me through the blood of Jesus, which means the sacrifice Jesus made for me washes away my sin and blemishes in the sight of God. God sees me as a part of His family, as someone who will spend eternity with Him. God sees me as a vessel of His love for the world.

As a follower of Jesus, there's even more to being kind to myself as I look back on my painful memories. What brings me the most hope in these moments is that I truly believe that God is *for* me. His Word says that He'll never leave me or abandon me.

Dr. Curt Thompson says, "Even though you cannot change the events of your story, you can change the way you experience your story."[5] The moment of hurt my dad brought into our family and into my life creeps its way into my thoughts about my marriage more than I'd like to admit. I mentioned earlier how often this moment of hurt comes up in counseling. For many years I was embarrassed by this and would proclaim, "Jamie, get it together!" every time the conversation moved to this moment of hurt for me.

Because I have experienced so much healing from therapy, I've been an advocate of counseling for a while now, and these last few years I have dedicated even more time to my mental health journey. During a group counseling session with my confessional community group[viii] where the pain from this wound once again showed up, I asked everyone, "When will this stop affecting me? When will I be healed from this?" Our counselor then gently reminded everyone (or mainly me), "There is no timeline for healing with Jesus."[ix] Tears filled my eyes. Although there were multiple people in the room, it felt like this statement was just for me. And I needed it to sink into not only my brain but also my heart.

On one hand, this truth is quite discouraging. "No timeline" means we don't have a finish line in view. "No timeline" means I could grapple and wrestle with this until the day I see Jesus face-to-face. I don't want that. I want this to be over. I want it to be fixed. I want to get it together. I want this wound stitched up and dealt with once and for all. I'm fine with a scar—I just want to quit dealing with an infected wound that needs more healing.

On the other hand, there is hope in this. Jesus is not giving up on me. "No timeline" means there's no threshold that I can reach where He is suddenly exhausted by me or too frustrated with me. He's not wondering when I'll get it together on this or when I'll stop bringing this pain to Him. There won't come a day when Jesus looks

viii. We meet monthly and help carry each other's burdens and have a counselor join us.
ix. Thank you, Dr. Curt Thompson, for being on this journey with me.

at the Father and the Spirit and declares that they have given too much of Themselves to me, and it's time to move on.

I've grown to realize that time doesn't heal all wounds. If you were banking on that, I am truly sorry to be the one to burst your bubble. On the flip side, I also believe that because of Jesus' work for us on the cross, these wounds, although they might never fully go away, don't get the final word in our lives. Wounds, pains, hurts, and terrible life circumstances might wound and scar us, but they don't define us. Our lives are marked by more than the choices we make or the circumstances we live in.

A NEW LENS

Our lives are marked by more than the choices we make or the circumstances we live in.

It's so much easier to believe God is near us and for us in easy, happy, joyful times. But when hard times and suffering come, when we're hurting, we sometimes feel very alone. There's a hard moment in Jesus' life where He felt very alone. He even felt as though His Father had abandoned Him (Matthew 27:46).

Hours before being arrested and crucified, Jesus went to the garden of Gethsemane with three of His disciples (Matthew 26; Mark 14; Luke 22). He urged them to stay awake and pray while He went into the garden to pray on His own. Jesus prayed, "'Father, if you are willing, remove this cup from me. Nevertheless, not my will, but yours, be done.' And there appeared to him an angel from heaven, strengthening him" (Luke 22:42–43). While Jesus was praying and begging God to make a different way for their plan to unfold, He was comforted by an angel. In His greatest moment of pain, when His disciples couldn't even keep their eyes open and He was about to endure one of the greatest miseries known to man—the crucifixion—He was not alone.

Jesus knew that this was part of God's plan—for Him and for all of God's people. He asked God to take His cup away but then said, "Nevertheless, not my will, but yours, be done." This night, this intense pain, was a part of Jesus' journey. Jesus responded by trusting His Father, and His Father responded by comforting Him.

Jesus knew there was good on the other side of that moment. He was in on the plan, after all. It was not a surprise to Him that He was about to take on the sins of humanity so that we can be in a restored relationship with God. And yet this was still a moment of pain.

What if we did the same? What if the right response to our moments of hurt and pain was to follow Jesus' example and lay them down at the feet of our Father? To give them back to Him. To trust that He has always been with us, that He's with us now, and that He will never leave us. To trust that He can handle our pain. What if we truly believed that our pain is not our burden to fully carry because we have a God who says we can bring our burdens to Him, and He will carry them for us (Matthew 11:28–29)?

As you have been reading, I'm confident you, too, know your moments of pain. Those moments aren't prone to hide from us. We can remember them easily. Today, take that pain to the Father and know you are not carrying this alone. The burden is not yours to shoulder alone. You are not walking this road alone.

Jesus did all things perfectly and without sin, and He shows us in Scripture how to respond to *our* moments of hurt, confusion, and pain. In her *Valleys* Bible study, Kat Armstrong says, "We can feel low because we have so many doubts and also be deep in trust. You see, when our valley of doubt feels like death, it may, in fact, be a cradle—the birthplace of a deeper faith. When you find yourself laid low, kneel, and remember that the soil is deep in these valleys—and deep soil makes for the best farmland. As you cultivate a life of faith, dig deep when you are in a valley. It's an opportunity to trust God with your giant-sized doubts."[6]

FOR OUR GOOD

I know in my heart that God uses all things for His glory. And I truly believe that He uses all things for our good (Romans 8:28). But in my few decades of life, I've endured some truly hard times. There's been pain I'd never want to revisit. Sorrow I'd never wish on anyone. Uncomfortable seasons in life and ministry. Painful seasons of disconnect in my marriage. Hard moments of parenting I want to put behind me for good. Decisions about work that made me regret being in charge. I once had Beth Moore on my podcast, and we talked about this exact thing. Beth made a bold statement that I have yet to forget. She said, "It is rarely under comfortable conditions that we will bear a lot of fruit."[7]

Jesus talked about this with His disciples in one of my favorite sections of Scripture. He said,

> "I am the true vine, and my Father is the vinedresser. Every branch in me that does not bear fruit he takes away, and every branch that does bear fruit he *prunes*, that it may bear more fruit. Already you are clean because of the word that I have spoken to you. Abide in me, and I in you. As the branch cannot bear fruit by itself, unless it abides in the vine, neither can you, unless you

abide in me. I am the vine; you are the branches. Whoever abides in me and I in him, he it is that bears much fruit, for apart from me you can do nothing."

JOHN 15:1–5, EMPHASIS ADDED

Did you catch that slightly painful part? God the Father often prunes us so that we may bear even more fruit.

In a vineyard, a vine grows grapes only when it's under stress. In non-stressful situations, there's just a vine full of leaves. They have no need for grapes, so they just grow ginormous, green, leafy vines, which might look beautiful, but they produce zero fruit. The people Jesus was speaking to would have been very familiar with the vineyard language. They would have seen vineyards around them, some of them might have even grown grapes themselves, and most of them would have been familiar with the way the Old Testament Scriptures frequently used the vineyard or vine as a symbol for Israel. By comparing us to branches, Jesus is letting us in on an uncomfortable truth: in seasons of pruning, He is cutting something away to produce something in us that couldn't have been produced otherwise.

There is fruit from the drought. There is fruit from the pain. There is fruit from the circumstances you didn't ask for. The moments of hurt, the things we endure, the painful years in our lives, and all the sorrow, grief, and loss are not wasted. Beth said it best in that interview: "All of it, to the last inch of it, mattered."

> **In seasons of pruning, He is cutting something away to produce something in us that couldn't have been produced otherwise.**

IT ALL MATTERS

I never want to gloss over or overspiritualize my wounds or yours. I never want to be the one saying, "It was all worth it, and I'd do it all over again," because to be honest with you, I wouldn't. Those early years of parenting four kids were so very hard for me. Beautiful fruit was produced in my life that couldn't have developed without that time, but I wouldn't want to experience it again.

I would never want for three of my children to have to start their lives with so much loss. I would never want to lose two babies to miscarriage, even if I was young and unmarried. I'd never want to endure the sorrow of laying down dreams to die. I'd never want to go through some of the hardest years of my marriage ever again. I'm sure you have your own list of things you would never choose to endure again. The fruit produced in our lives reveals to us the worth, but there are things we don't wish to do again. We can say for sure that "God made it matter."[x] Friend, there is hope and joy in knowing that it all mattered. The pain, the trials, the loss—every circumstance—mattered because God made it matter.

What would your life be like if you could look back on your circumstances—on your pain, sorrow, fear, moments of hurt, and poor decision-making—and see them through a different lens? A lens of compassion for the growth you hadn't yet had. A lens of grace for the things you didn't know. A lens of gratefulness for the growth God would produce in you through that trial. What if we walked through current dark days and looked back on past dark days through this whole new lens?

I encourage you to look back on your past with kindness

---

x. Another brilliant quote from Beth Moore in that same podcast interview!

toward yourself. Start today by pulling up that empty chair and imagining your wounded self sitting next to you. Imagine them carrying the pain of circumstances, the shame of mistakes, the sorrow of grief, and have compassion for them. Speak kind words over your past self. Let your past self know that you see them and you believe in them.

The pain, the trials, the loss—every circumstance—mattered because God made it matter.

Remind yourself that you are not alone now, you were not alone then, and you never will be.

My friend Mary Marantz recently said this on her Instagram account: "There is this version of you that you became in order to survive. Be kind to her. She was doing the best she could with what she had at the time. . . . Be gentle with her. Make friends with her. But also maybe introduce her to this new version you are becoming. I think she'll be so proud of how far you've come."[8]

I know it sounds crazy, but trust me, it's healing. Believe with all your heart and mind that in those moments of hurt, poor choices, circumstances you didn't choose, and all the other ways you have felt pain over the years, you were not alone in them. God has been with you through them all. God has loved you through them all. Be kind to yourself when looking back on your days.

PONDER YOUR PAST AND PRESENT HURTS

Pray

Father, as I look back on my years and see pain, I also see You. As I look back on my years and see sorrow, I also see You. As I look back on my years and see poor choices, I also see You. You have always been with me, and I find so much comfort in knowing that You never abandoned me. You actually came near to me. I find so much comfort and peace in knowing that for all the things I've endured, You have made them matter. Amen.

Reflect

Name your past or present hurts. How does this hurt impact your current reality?

_____

_____

_____

_____

_____

What is it that you are looking back on that constantly makes you feel as though you will never have it all together?

_____

_____

_____

_____

_____

Consider your past or present sin. How are you being kind to yourself? How could you be kinder to yourself?

_____

_____

_____

_____

How can you see your past or present hurt through a lens of trusting God that He has made (or will make) it matter? Is this something you already believe or need help to believe?

_____

_____

_____

_____

CHAPTER 5

LET IT GO

PONDER YOUR OBLIGATIONS

I remember exactly where I was when I said yes when I most definitely should have told a friend no.

Years ago my friend called me and poured her heart out about a new ministry she wanted to start. As she shared idea after idea, I walked laps around my small backyard. Pacing and listening. Pacing and talking. I grew more intrigued with every minute that passed. I loved this friend and valued all her work in our community and the world through the organization she had started. But this call was about something new in addition to the ministry she was already doing.

I'll be honest, I was surprised when she asked me. We were friends and all, but this role was above my pay grade. I hadn't done anything like this before. I wasn't doing the type of public speaking I do now. I had a baby podcast that I had just started, and there were no books with my name on the cover. I listened as she shared her dreams that day. I felt like she was on the verge of something fabulous, and I knew I wanted to be a part of it. Before she could even finish asking me if I wanted to join, I screamed, "Yes! Yes! Yes!!!"

I walked into the house with a bit of pep in my step. I was so excited to be joining her journey. She's a leader, a dreamer, and a visionary, and I would follow her to the ends of the earth. When I shared all of this with my husband, he was excited for me as well. So I went to my calendar and marked down the date for when she wanted to meet again. I was about to start an exciting new adventure! I'd been feeling like God was up to something new in my world, and this surely must be it!

There was just one problem. One gigantic problem. A few days later, I started to feel that nudge that happens inside—the one that's really the Holy Spirit helping you out. That gentle reminder. That feeling of knowing something is off. I'm used to that feeling now, and I still wish it didn't show up as often as it does.

You see, what my friend didn't know (because I didn't disclose it) is that just a few weeks before our conversation, I'd made a commitment to myself and God about my time. I was parenting four kids under age ten; trying to produce a podcast in my "spare" time; volunteering at my church, the kids' school, and the high school in our neighborhood; and speaking to and encouraging moms at MOPS[i] groups around town every once in a while. I was at my capacity, and I knew it.

At that time, I had just finished *The Best Yes* by Lysa TerKeurst, and something in that book prompted me to make a list of what I would say yes to in the coming months. Here's what I wrote on that list:

---

i. Mothers of Preschoolers!

- My kids and family
- Volunteering at church, Reagan High School, and my children's school
- Speaking and podcasting opportunities

Those were the only things on my list. I would give my time to my people, my church, my community, and my new podcasting and speaking opportunities. It seemed simple enough as I wrote it all out, especially because I wasn't getting exciting calls to start new things with awesome people daily.

But then I got the phone call from my friend—the one I immediately said yes to. The Spirit nudged me to remember my list. I found myself in a pickle.[ii] I had already given her my yes, which, believe it or not, means a lot to me. But in doing so, I'd unintentionally gone back on the commitment I had made to myself, my family, and God.

Can you relate to this moment? The time when you have, once again, overextended yourself and your life with obligations—the things you said that you would do. This moment will forever be a marker for me, a reminder that I'm only one person and that I can do only so much.

PERMISSION TO SAY NO

Many of us are constantly overwhelmed and overextended, stuck in the "can't get it together" space. When I titled this book *Why Can't I Get It Together?*, I knew that this was the message many

---

ii. If that phrase is new to you, it means that I found myself stuck. We say things like this in the South.

readers would expect. Hopefully, now that you have done some personal inventory and reflection, you know that your ability to get it together is so much more than juggling your to-do list and dealing with overcommitting to obligations.

Thankfully, the struggle of saying yes when I should have said no isn't a huge problem for me anymore. Maturing a lot in my faith has helped. I've found my lane with my work passions, and I have grown to understand what I'm gifted at and what I'm not. I don't say that as someone who has arrived at perfection but as someone who no longer feels this tension as much in my life. When I look back at times when I have felt overwhelmed and overextended by obligations, it's usually because I was living out of a sense of fear.

I fear I won't get asked again.
I fear I'll be overlooked next time.
I fear no one will like me.
I fear this is my one chance at anything big, fun, or exciting.

I was talking to another friend who struggles with this often, and she shared that her willingness to overextend herself was because she wants to be loved. She struggles with saying no to a friend's request and then wondering if that person would still love her.

I looked at her straight in the eyes and said, "You know you have permission to say no."

She paused and replied, "Actually, I don't feel like I do." That's what it is for so many of us. We think we can't say no to things for several reasons.

- We won't be loved.
- We will miss the opportunity.

- We can do it better than everyone else.
- We don't think anyone else will say yes.
- We want to keep up the appearance of being awesome.

When I said yes to the exciting ministry project that wasn't on my "yes" list, I knew that I couldn't commit to this project, even though it sounded amazing. I tried to convince myself a hundred times over that surely that *cute little* list I had made wasn't in charge of me. I tend not to like to be told what to do, especially from a list that no one knew about but me. I hadn't even told my husband about the list! I could have moved forward with the project, and the only person who knew about the conflict would be me. Well, me and Jesus!

But I couldn't. My soul wouldn't let me. That Holy Spirit feeling wouldn't let me. I had made that list for a reason, and this moment was proof of why I so desperately needed it. I was willing to say yes to all the things so I wouldn't miss a great opportunity. I felt that there were new things on the horizon for me, and I feared that if I told my friend no, she would never invite me to anything ever again. (What a shallow view of my friendship with her!)

I spent a few days thinking about it and trying to convince myself that I could say yes. I justified this as a big opportunity, and big opportunities don't come along every day. I convinced myself that I would hold true to my "yes" list *next* time. I tried and tried to work myself out of my commitment to my list, but at the end of the day, I just couldn't. There was no way around or under or over this list. I had to face it straight on for what it was: my commitment.

I called my friend and told her about my dumb list and how I had committed to myself and to God to stay true to it in this season. I felt stupid. I mean, who screams yes excitedly and then calls back to turn it down because of something she wrote in her journal? This girl. Of course, my amazing, loving friend completely understood (even if she was bummed), and I hung up the phone bummed but also very proud of myself. And to this day, I still get to partner with that friend on numerous occasions. I didn't lose my one shot.

———

There are many reasons you might think you can't say no, and yet deep down, you know your life would have more meaning, you'd be more rested, and your yes would be more impactful if you would pick a thing or two and let it go.[iii] One of the hardest things to do in life is to prioritize what matters, but it's one of the most impactful. And the impact is more lasting than you can imagine.

Different seasons of life have their own schedules, demands, and opportunities. Different seasons will also bring up different *responses* to those schedules, demands, and opportunities. That is why it's so important not to neglect your Reality Inventory, which shows what your life demands of you in *this* season—your current reality.

Your life—your past and present hurts, obligations, needs, desires, expectations, and responsibilities—requires balance. Your obligations are the things you say you will do for yourself and those around you. There are only so many hours in the day, and there's only so much of you to go around. Saying yes to too many things will throw off the balance of your reality. When your obligations are out of whack, the other areas of your reality will suffer. It might mean that you can't take care of all your responsibilities or that you aren't able to take care of your physical needs.

———

iii. Cue the Idina Menzel karaoke moment!

Our relationship with God is the fountain from which our responses will flow. The responses are a result of that relationship, and when it is deep, intimate, and rich, the right responses to our current reality flow effortlessly from us. But when the balance of our reality is way off, all relationships in our life suffer, especially our first relationship—with our Father. When that relationship is strained, neglected, or forgotten, our responses to our reality come from a place of fear, anxiety, and loneliness. When the areas of our reality are out of balance, our world feels completely out of control.

Our relationship with God is the fountain from which our responses will flow.

"Living under the weight of unhealthy obligations is like carrying an emotional debt made up of a million unspoken assumptions. The debt stealthily piles up over time and slowly silences your voice, leaving you wondering if you are just meant to grin and bear it through this life."[1] And I'd add to that, leaving you feeling as if you can never get it together.

So limit the yeses. Prioritize your relationship with God over the obligations. Remember that your real friends will still love you after you say no. And know without a doubt that God loves you in the yeses, the nos, the maybes, and everything in between.

WHO ARE YOU?

I remember when I first started going to church, the question of whether someone was "more like Mary or Martha" was so intriguing to me. I wasn't sure who I was more like, or even who I was supposed to be most like!

In Luke 10, sisters Mary and Martha welcome Jesus into their home.

> Now as they went on their way, Jesus entered a village. And a woman named Martha welcomed him into her house. And she had a sister called Mary, who sat at the Lord's feet and listened to his teaching. But Martha was distracted with much serving. And she went up to him and said, "Lord, do you not care that my sister has left me to serve alone? Tell her then to help me." But the Lord answered her, "Martha, Martha, you are anxious and troubled about many things, but one thing is necessary. Mary has chosen the good portion, which will not be taken away from her."
>
> (vv. 38–42)

Martha welcomed Jesus into her house and then got down to business serving everyone. She was doing what she knew best, and it wasn't wrong. Before long, she realized that she was serving alone, and this bothered her, because Mary was with Jesus soaking up every word He was saying.

What we need to see in this story isn't about serving or not serving. Personally, I would much rather be Mary—among all the guys hanging out in the living room—than in the kitchen cooking any day. But this isn't about hanging out, cooking, or who is having more fun—which Jesus made abundantly clear when He lovingly rebuked Martha about what she was asking Him to do. Jesus pointed out that Mary's posture of listening, learning, and *being with* Jesus was the only thing necessary at that moment. He was totally aware that dinner needed to be served. He knew that a house full of guests required some work. But He insisted that Mary's devotion to Him was the most important thing in that moment and it would not be taken away.

Who are you: Martha or Mary? Not "Would you rather serve or be served?" and not "Where do you feel more comfortable—in the kitchen or in the living room?" Neither of those. Step back a bit and really examine yourself. Are you more concerned with all the items on your to-do list, or are you more concerned about *being with* Jesus?

Jesus was constantly offering a different way of living to His followers then, and He still extends this offer to us today. A life full of anxiety and worry cannot produce the fruit we want to see in our lives. So often we push ourselves to our maximum capacity and beyond with too many yeses. Jesus offers a different path. He offers a path of rest and rejuvenation through Him. He said it Himself: "Come to me, all who labor and are heavy laden, and I will give you rest. Take my yoke upon you, and learn from me, for I am gentle and lowly in heart, and you will find rest for your souls. For my yoke is easy, and my burden is light" (Matthew 11:28–30).

So often we push ourselves to our maximum capacity and beyond with too many yeses. Jesus offers a different path.

PONDER YOUR OBLIGATIONS

Pray

Father, as I look at my time and my obligations, I want to honor You in all that I do. Please help me to evaluate my yeses and my nos. Please help me find a way to include You in my day and not overextend myself so much that I don't rest with You. Thank You for creating a pathway to living where You are present and with us.

I want to choose to trust in Your plans for my life and not try to fill my days with so many obligations that I neglect a relationship with You. You bring me peace and comfort, and I will choose to trust You with my current reality. Amen.

Reflect

Do you struggle to say no to commitments? If so, what feeling or thought is behind that struggle? Why do you think you can't say no?

_____

_____

_____

_____

_____

Look back at your Reality Inventory. After reading about obligations, have your thoughts or feelings about anything you listed changed? If so, what has changed?

_____

_____

_____

_____

_____

Reread Jesus' words at the end of this chapter about His yoke. Respond to His words. Does your life reflect that you believe Him?

_____

_____

_____

_____

_____

Make a list of the three to five areas of life where you will say yes to asks from others in this season. Are there any obligations you want to let go of today?

_____

_____

_____

_____

CHAPTER 6

A VERY GOOD GIFT

PONDER YOUR PHYSICAL NEEDS

My husband, Aaron, and I recently vacationed in New York City. When we visit it often leaves us wondering if we could be city people or if we should stick to the semi-country life in our log cabin on a few acres outside of Austin.

Our NYC hotel had a mini basketball court inside. Everything is so compact in the city that this was surprising! I played basketball in high school, and apparently, one night on our trip, I thought I was still sixteen-year-old Jamie and not forty-four-year-old Jamie. While Aaron set up the Scrabble board in the lobby (yes, you read that right, we play Scrabble on vacation), I decided to shoot some hoops.

Everything was going great until it wasn't. Aaron walked in to tell me that our board was ready, and, perhaps wanting to show off in front of my man, I went in for a layup. It was as if the whole world started moving in slow motion. I tripped over my boots (yes, I had on boots while thinking I could shoot hoops), fell on my knees, and then my dress (yes, a dress) flew up in the air. Aaron ran over to see if I was okay, trying to show concern and not laugh hysterically as he helped me to my feet and smoothed down my dress since I wasn't the only one shooting hoops that night!

I was fine and spent the rest of our trip hobbling through the city and putting ice on my knees at night. I was reminded once again that my body is not what it used to be, and it has very specific needs. It took me about a month to visit my doctor once I returned home because even though one of my knees was still hurting, I didn't have the time to take care of myself.

I know that taking care of my body matters, but often, even when there's pain involved, I put the needs of my body behind every other need, desire, obligation, and responsibility I might have. I don't think I would have said out loud that I thought my body didn't matter, but my actions sure reflected that mindset.

OUR BODIES

You know that feeling in your head when something seems too massive to comprehend and your brain hurts a little? That happens to me when I think about the human body. It is so intricate and complex! Our bodies are miracles, beautiful pieces of art. I'm grateful to have lived this long and not had any major health issues, but I have many friends who have journeyed through some hard times with their bodies: breast cancer, strokes, infertility, autoimmune disease, and so much more. When I hear how their bodies often fight to heal themselves, I'm amazed. And when I hear how some have to adjust their lives to care for their diseased, broken, or healing bodies, I'm in awe of their discipline and dedication.

As a busy woman, I often put the needs of my body on a back burner due to the ever-present needs in front of me. I don't know what it is about women, but we often place our needs behind those of everyone else in our lives. I realize I'm making a sweeping generalization here, but I have seen this so often in friends' lives and in my own life—we'll make sure everyone around us has had their yearly checkups and gets to their therapies on time, all while neglecting our own checkups and needs. We care deeply about the bodies of those around us while neglecting the body that God has gifted us personally. I don't think anyone wakes up and consciously decides to disregard the gift of their body. I don't think we're trying to think less of what God has said is good. I think we're simply viewing the needs of our body through a different lens. My friend Jess says, "The way we view our bodies is not a shallow, surface issue for the immature or the vain. The way we view our bodies is a deeply spiritual issue because our bodies are made by God, in the image of God, and they are where we encounter God for now."[1]

Your body matters. I want you to think about that for a minute. Whether you live in an abled body or a disabled body, a large body or a small body, a healthy body or an unhealthy body, your body matters, and the choices you make for your physical and mental health deserve your attention. This will look different for everyone, so there's no prescription for how to do this. But I can tell you that when you have the right response to your current reality, you can get it together, no matter what your body is telling you that it needs, wants, or demands.

I see this in my friends who live with bodies that don't seem to cooperate as they would like. One friend endured a stroke as a young woman, and her body will never be like it was before the stroke until she meets Jesus. Another friend lost her hearing as a

WHY CAN'T I GET IT TOGETHER?

Whether you live in an abled body or a disabled body, a large body or a small body, a healthy body or an unhealthy body, your body matters, and the choices you make for your physical and mental health deserve your attention.

young child, and she lives daily without something I often take for granted. Still another friend had a mastectomy and has had many challenges since that life-saving surgery. One has debilitating migraines. Another has PCOS, and her many flare-ups leave her feeling out of control and frustrated. The attention that these friends have to give their bodies makes a huge difference in their overall health and ability to function in the world. There is not a selfish bone in their bodies when they take time to rest and heal so that they can bring their best selves to their families, jobs, churches, and communities. Their right response to their current realities—faithfully caring for the many needs of their bodies—allows them to feel and know that they've got it together even though our world and our culture (and some people) might say otherwise.

A GOOD GIFT

If we lack the ability to see our bodies as good, we will lack the ability to see our bodies as something to be stewarded. Genesis 1:27 says, "So God created man in his own image, in the image of God he created him; male and female he created them." We were created as image bearers to the Father. Because God created us in His own image, our bodies are perfect. Being created in His image brings value into our lives—all of our lives—our bodies, minds, and souls.

My attitude toward my body has a great deal of impact on how much I feel I can get it together on any given day. Notice I didn't say the size of my body or the look of my body. Nope. You won't hear that from me. The way I view my body can alter how *together* I feel. If I view my body for what it can do for me, I move toward feeling out of control or chaotic. But if I view my body as a precious gift from the Lord that needs to be stewarded, cared for, acknowledged, loved, and rested, I can feel secure and controlled. If the size or look of our bodies determined our ability to get it together, we would all be in trouble. There isn't one size, shape, or color—so who would be the judge of this?

When we see our bodies as gifts, then we understand that we are receivers and that Someone is the Giver. God created us. He put His breath into humans. The psalmist says, "Know that the LORD, he is God! It is he who made us, and we are his; we are his people, and the sheep of his pasture" (Psalm 100:3). God is the giver of our lives, bodies, and souls. And we know that God gives good gifts (Matthew 7:11).

When we see that each of our bodies is very good and was created and gifted by God (Genesis 1:31), we understand that our bodies deserve our care and attention because that's how you treat a good gift. Culture would tell us that attention to our bodies means we strive to look a certain way, dress a certain way, or weigh a certain amount. But caring for our bodies as gifts means acknowledging the gifts and stewarding them well. I feel the most out of control and unable to get it together regarding the needs of my body when I'm trying to fit *my* body into what the world tells me it should be. That's the wrong response. The right response is to understand that I am

> **When we see that each of our bodies is very good and was created and gifted by God (Genesis 1:31), we understand that our bodies deserve our care and attention because that's how you treat a good gift.**

the workmanship of God, and He has prepared amazing things for me to do (Ephesians 2:10).

One of the best ways to care for the needs of our bodies is to pay attention to them and to rest when needed. God became our ultimate example of this when He created Sabbath for us. As God was creating everything, He said it was all good, and then He rested when He was done (Genesis 2:2–3). It's not about resting our souls, minds, and bodies to earn God's love or to check a box. We choose to rest because God offers it to us, He modeled it for us, and He says it's best for us. Again, what a gift from our good Father— rest that isn't about earning anything from God but rather is a gift to help us continue the good work that He has prepared for us. Rebekah Lyons says, "We are restless when we rest less."[2] Have you ever felt like your body isn't responding well to your current lifestyle or pace? For me, it's the emergence of fever blisters on my lips when I'm sick or stressed. I'm not saying that rest would heal my body of fever blisters, but those moments of illness or stress signal to me that I need to take care of my body, even if life feels chaotic or out of control.

Recently, our entire family played pickleball together for the first time. I am highly competitive and want to win at everything I do, so on the drive home, I was complaining about how I didn't win a single game that day. Everyone in my family beat me. My son looked at me seriously and replied, "Mom, you do know you have a bad back and that it just might not be in your cards anymore to win at everything you do." As much as I wanted to be offended, he was right. My body can't do what it used to do. The high school athlete is long gone. Long runs and CrossFit gyms used to be my friends, but heating pads and muscle relaxers have replaced them. Taking care of the needs of our bodies is not a one-size-fits-all endeavor. My current reality and season of life look different from yours. Evaluating your specific needs will help you determine what this looks like for you. Be honest with yourself when evaluating your needs. Take inventory of your current life and what you need. That might be realizing you can't stay up as late anymore. Or maybe you need to eat less dairy than when you were fifteen. Or maybe, like me, you have a slew of doctors' appointments to make because you are suddenly at the age of needing everything looked at!

I don't know what your specific needs are. But I do know that your body is a gift to be stewarded well. It matters deeply to your Father, and you should care for it and give it rest. And the best example you have of how to do this is in your Savior and friend, Jesus.

JESUS WAS NEEDY

Christmas and Easter are when we speak most about Jesus' earthly body—when we talk about His birth and His death. We often romanticize the coming of Jesus. Our nativity scenes are serene and shiny, but the reality was that a young pregnant woman rode a very long way on a donkey only to have to deliver her first child without a bed, family, or midwife in a barn surrounded by animals with her brand-new husband. Both entering the world and exiting the world were traumatic and difficult for our Savior. But more than that, we need to remember that Jesus didn't just wrap flesh around His

God-body; Jesus *became* flesh. He emptied Himself and entered into our world by being born in the likeness of man (Philippians 2:7).

Jesus became man, and therefore, He had human needs. Jesus was fully God and fully human, experiencing the same things we experience in our human bodies (Colossians 1:15–16; John 17:24; John 1:1–3; 1 Corinthians 8:6; Galatians 4:4). I'm not sure what's harder for you to imagine: Jesus being fully God or Jesus being fully human. As I think of Him being fully human, I'm encouraged that Jesus understands some of our own personal, unique challenges. For us, on this side of Scripture, His humanity might be harder for us to comprehend. But when Jesus walked on earth, no one questioned His humanity. It was the opposite for them. They questioned His God-ness. They walked with Him, talked with Him, hugged Him, felt His hand on their shoulders, and smiled at Him—those things were never questioned. What was questioned was His deity.

Jesus said, "I and the Father are one" (John 10:30), and immediately, the Jews picked up stones to stone Him for blasphemy. Everyone could clearly see His humanity, but His deity was harder to comprehend for many. But it's so important for us, as followers of Jesus, to lean into both parts of Jesus. And because He was fully human, we can be assured that His body also had needs, just like ours.

Let's start with that less-than-romantic delivery among the animals. You don't have to be a mom to know that babies are the neediest and most vulnerable of all humans. There's nothing, and I mean *nothing*, a baby can do on their own. They can't comfort themselves. They can't feed themselves. They can't clean themselves. Nothing. I would have completely understood if Jesus just appeared one day from the mountains and walked Himself into Nazareth as a grown person. He would have skipped out on all the newborn vulnerability because He's God—and does God really need to make Himself vulnerable? Yet He did.

When we think about the needs that our bodies uniquely experience, we can't forget that Jesus understands this. For many years, He completely depended on His mother, Mary, for *all* His needs. Imagine that. Jesus, God with flesh, needed His mommy to care for Him. Mary tucked him in at night, made His breakfast, kissed His boo-boos, and even potty trained Him! I'm blown away each time I imagine that. Jesus was needy. His body was needy.

So many of you have bodily needs that feel overwhelming. And when you experience debilitating days and can't meet your responsibilities or commitments, you can begin to feel defeated, out of control, or overwhelmed. On these days, remember Jesus' response to His body's needs. Remember that Jesus, on the way to His crucifixion, exhausted and already near death, needed someone to help Him carry His cross (Luke 23:26). He needed help. Although I'm certain none of you currently need help carrying your cross to your death, I know that some of you need help to do other things because your bodies are not capable of finishing the task. Remember, Jesus understands.

We see Jesus, our Savior, experience other bodily pains that we do understand and experience regularly. In the book of John, when Jesus interacted with the woman at the well, He confessed His weariness and then sat down to rest (4:6). I have often breezed past this section excited to get to my favorite part where He offers this woman living water, missing this moment to see Jesus' humanity so clearly. Jesus was weary. I would never choose to experience weariness if I didn't have to. If I were fully God and fully human, I would totally pull my God card when I was tired! I'd want to be invincible. I'd want to be able to do *all* the things in life. But not Jesus. He was weary, and He responded to His weariness with rest.

How often do you and I feel weariness in our bodies and fail or refuse to take the time to rest? We feel like there are too many important things to do, and there's not enough time to stop and rest. But Jesus Christ had the most important job to do—bringing eternal salvation to humanity through His perfect life and sacrificial death. Tell me whatever you are doing is more important than that! Jesus was fully aware of the need to care for His body. He and His disciples had been walking all over Judea and Galilee, so Jesus took the time to rest His body. Dr. Saundra Dalton-Smith says, "If you only rest when the work is done, you will never feel you have permission to rest."[3] I *always* feel that there's more work to be done. Jesus knew what His future held. In this story about the woman at the well, Jesus knew He had so much more work to do, and still, He rested.

In Matthew 8, we see Jesus go on a healing spree. First, He healed a man with leprosy, then a servant, Peter's mother-in-law, many who were demon-possessed, and many more who were sick. It was exhausting work, for sure. In response, Jesus got in a boat and took a nap. It was such a deep nap, in fact, that a storm began and didn't even wake Him (v. 24). (That's my favorite kind of nap— where you wake up and don't know what day it is or where you are!) Jesus was exhausted, and we know there was also so much work ahead of Him. But Jesus didn't push through the exhaustion. He didn't try to go and go and go until He couldn't go anymore. He rested. His right response to His reality was to rest.

PONDER YOUR PHYSICAL NEEDS

Pray
Jesus, as I consider the needs that my body has, I find great comfort in knowing You, too, had needs. You understand my weariness, and You understand my need for help. Will You help me

trust You with my body—to care for it and to love it? Will You help me adjust my heart's posture toward this gift You have given me? Jesus, thank You for showing me how to care for my body. Amen.

Reflect

How do you struggle to know your needs versus your desires?

_____

_____

_____

_____

_____

_____

Are you grateful for the gift of your body? How do you see and care for your body as a gift?

_____

_____

_____

_____

_____

_____

Describe your current relationship with rest and Sabbath. Does this need to change, and if so, how?

_____

_____

_____

_____

_____

How does knowing that Jesus was needy and experienced exhaustion and bodily pain affect the way you see Him or relate to Him?

_____

_____

_____

_____

CHAPTER 7

THE GOOD, THE BAD, AND THE TWISTED

PONDER YOUR DESIRES

Though you may have a hard time identifying your physical needs, I guarantee that none of you will have difficulty identifying your desires. It doesn't matter what age you are or what season of life you are currently in, you have desires. Mine started at an early age.

In the third grade, I desired glasses so badly that I bought a pair of fake glasses from a kiosk at the mall. A few years later, my eyesight changed, and I *had* to get glasses, but by then, the cool factor was gone.[i] After *having* to wear glasses for a few years, all I wanted were contacts!

In middle school I desired to save myself sexually until marriage, but then high school hit, and those desires changed drastically.

---

i. In seventh grade, my glasses broke when a basketball slammed into my face, and when my dad fixed them with super glue, he accidentally got his gluey finger stuck on a lens. Afterward I had to wear glasses with a permanent fingerprint on them. He was literally with me at all times. And I'm not sure these fixed glasses were any better than the broken ones.

79

I simply wanted to feel loved no matter what. My desires felt confusing and led me down a destructive path.

I ran track in high school, and it lit a renewed fire in me into adulthood. I began to love running for exercise in my early thirties. It was great stress relief, something to keep me in shape *and* give me a little bit of alone time as a mom to young kids. I ran my first half-marathon in Nashville, Tennessee, and I was hooked. The training was hard and time-consuming, but the rush I got as I crossed the finish line after 13.1 miles made me want to start training again immediately.[ii] And I did. I ran that race again and then competed in three more half-marathons until I noticed that it was getting harder to train because of some back issues. When I found out I have degenerative disc disease, the doctor recommended that I not run anymore. I wanted so badly to finish a full marathon, but that dream was taken from me. Since the diagnosis, I've tried to run a few times again, but each time I make it only a few weeks before my back demands that I stop. I'm now a walker and love walking. But I'd be lying if I said I never dreamed of that full marathon. Sadly, that desire will most likely never be a reality for me.

Currently in my life, I have a desire that I feel afraid to say out loud for a few reasons. First, if it never happens, what will I make of these years of desiring this? Second, if you all think this is a dumb desire, then what does it do for me to say it out loud? Some of you have these same desires. Maybe, like me, you are not the youngest kid on the block, and so these desires feel scary. I have two desires in my life that couldn't be more different, and I have no idea if either one of them will ever come true. I'd love to own a bookstore and wine bar in my cute little town, and I'd love to have my own TV

---

ii. You know, I even had the *13.1* sticker on the back of my minivan. I was one of *those* people.

show. I told you, they are massively different, and yet my heart has been set on them both for years. I have no idea if either will ever come to fruition, but they each hold a spot inside my heart.

As humans we have experienced confusing desires since the beginning of time. Wanting glasses, wanting to be loved, career goals, and running a marathon are not bad desires. Honestly, most of my desires in life wouldn't be classified as *bad* at all. For me, this is where trusting God with my desires can sometimes get difficult. I'm not asking for a million dollars to fall into my lap or desiring a new husband. I want my kids to love Jesus. I want to excel in my career, to maybe own a bookstore one day, and to have a vacation with my man each year. Oh, and that TV show I dream of hosting would be nice too!

If you're reading along and having a hard time figuring out what it is that you desire, ask yourself, *What do I find myself daydreaming about?* Where your mind wanders when it has space to dream is a good place to start. I find myself daydreaming about reading books, interviewing guests, growing old with my man, and seeing all my kids following Jesus.

I asked some friends to share things they desire:

"I want to be a good mom and for my kids to know Jesus."

"I want to own a home where I can stay at home with my new baby and make memories there for years to come."

"I want to have a healthy and reliable body, but it would also be nice to lose a few pounds."

"I want more affection from my husband."

"I want financial freedom that would allow me to focus on my love of writing."

"I want another child and the ability to homeschool my family when the time comes."

I wouldn't consider any of those to be bad desires or things they shouldn't desire. In fact, a lot of those desires are on my list as well.

Think back to your Reality Inventory. What popped into your mind as you thought about your own desires? Now consider your response to this desire. Sometimes taking a deeper look into what we desire helps us figure out where this desire is coming from. Desires are not bad, but would you say that this desire is overwhelming other areas of your life? Here are some questions to reflect on as you consider your response to your desire.

ARE YOUR DESIRES ALL-CONSUMING?

When we were in the middle of the adoption process to bring two of our kids home from another country, I was completely consumed with the process. And rightly so—we were dealing with my kids' lives! Because of how the adoption process worked then, we were considered our kids' legal parents in their home country *way* before the US considered us their new parents. Imagine being separated from your kids by an ocean and a five-hour flight, and there's nothing you can do about it. The desire to have my children home was a good desire, and it came from a great place. But that desire began to take over my life, consuming it in ways that made other areas of my life unbearable. I often felt chaotic and that there was no chance of getting it together because this one area of my reality was so consuming. I'm not saying this wasn't a big deal or something I shouldn't have cared about. But it's important for us to evaluate our desires and the way they can overwhelm us— even the good desires. Because if we have the right response to our current reality (my reality was two kids at home and two kids in another country), then we can feel like we have it together, no matter what is happening.

IS YOUR DESIRE THE FOUNDATION OF YOUR FAITH?

Or put another way, is your faith dependent on your desire becoming a reality? Have you had conversations with God about what you desire? They can sometimes go like this: "God, if You give me a baby, I'll follow You forever." "God, if You get me through this anatomy and physiology class,[iii] I'll follow You forever." "God, if You bring me a husband, we'll be the best Christians ever!"

As we were waiting on our kids to come home, I often wanted to make deals with God about the timeline of them joining our family. "God, if you bring my kids home this month, I will know for sure that You are real." It felt as though I was basing my faith journey on how quickly He came through with His end of the deal.

When we do this, we become "god," and He becomes a slave to our desires. God is not a genie in a bottle here to grant us all the things we desire. God is not holding out on us, nor does He think our desires are necessarily wrong and evil. If God being real to you depends on Him giving you your desires, then your faith is built on sinking sand. God is the only One who gets everything He wants. "Many are the plans in a person's heart, but it is the LORD's purpose that prevails" (Proverbs 19:21 NIV). God's purposes for you, what He wants in your life, might not line up with the plans of your heart—and even so, He is still good, right, true, and worthy of all honor and praise.

---

iii. Fun fact: I took this class three times in college before I passed.

DO YOUR DESIRES DETERMINE GOD'S LOVE FOR YOU?

We don't like to acknowledge this one to be true, and yet for so many of us, this is how we respond to God. When we petition God for our desires day after day, month after month, year after year, and there's still no movement from God, we wonder, *Has He abandoned me? Does He hear me? Where is He in my life?*

In the adoption process, when I was waiting for my kids to come home, I struggled to see God as loving and good when my desires were not fulfilled. I wanted my kids to be home *immediately*, but unfortunately, that wasn't the way He brought them home. I often found my heart wondering if God saw us or even loved us, because if He loved me, and if He loved my kids, He would surely bring them home. It only made sense to bring them home immediately. I still have no idea why it took two and a half years to bring my son home, but I do trust in the goodness of God in the midst of that unmet desire.

GOOD DESIRE

When you respond to your current reality from a place of intimacy with God, your response will reflect the love, trust, and security of that deep and abiding relationship. When you respond to your current reality from any place other than a deep relationship with your Father, your response will reflect fear, distrust, anxiety, or a lack of security. When our desires—even the good ones—become overemphasized in our current reality, it throws off the balance of our reality. If the desire to be married, graduate from seminary, start your own business, have your kids love the Lord, or travel the world become all-consuming, you can feel out of control and completely unable to get it together. Your thoughts become overcrowded, your emotions start to take over, and your body begins to alert you that something is off.

When the desire area of our current reality is out of proportion, we become consumed by those wants and begin to wonder where God is when the wants aren't being fulfilled. Even good desires can become idols—something we prize more than God—when they begin to dominate our thoughts, time, and energy.

Desiring marriage is a good thing—but when you are thinking about it more than about following and doing the will of God, it has become an idol. Desiring children is a good thing—but when you begin to feel as though you will be blessed by God more with children than without children, it has become an idol. Desiring a better job is a good thing—but when you think your value will finally matter, it has become an idol. When good desires get twisted and then seat themselves on the throne of your heart, it is impossible to get it together.

> **Even good desires can become idols—something we prize more than God—when they begin to dominate our thoughts, time, and energy.**

When this happens, we look at our current realities and assume God has abandoned us or is choosing to be far from us. But neither is true. I have friends who desire marriage and, year after year, are still single. I have friends longing to be parents, and God still hasn't opened their wombs. I have friends desiring to know what is next in their career path and still not feeling certain about what is next. I have friends desiring to stay holy in their singleness and wondering if it is really worth it. I'm so encouraged by watching all of these friends fight for the right responses to their desires and seeing their faith and steadfastness.

God blesses us by meeting some of our desires and wants in this life, but often, even when He does, something in us isn't entirely fulfilled. We are still wanting something, and it's something that only He can provide.

Right now, look back at the desire you wrote down in your Reality Inventory (p. 34). What is the root of your desire? Take a moment right now to talk to God about your desire and ask Him to fulfill the root of your desire in the perfect way that only He can. Ask for His help to have a right response to your desire and trust Him with the outcome of your desire.

ULTIMATE DESIRE

There was a time in my life when I desperately wanted God to give me the desires of my heart, and I was almost certain He would because I had followed Him into an uncertain place like He had asked me to. In 2011, I was a stay-at-home mom to my four kids with no job change on the horizon when suddenly I found myself in a brand-new career as a morning show host at one of the local country radio stations here in Austin.[iv] It was the dream job I never knew to dream of. But it was short-lived because my kids needed me more than ever, and I felt that God was asking me to lay it down, so I did.

One year later, an opportunity popped up to get back into radio.

---

iv. I share this whole story in my book *You Be You*. I won a contest to become a DJ—for real. A *contest*!

I felt so seen by God, and I just knew that *this* was my chance. My desire had never gone away. I longed to get back behind a microphone and on the radio. But as I considered the opportunity, I couldn't shake the feeling that it wasn't what I was supposed to be doing, and after much discussion, the job wasn't available anymore.

I had made an internal deal with God when I quit the radio station. I would follow Him and lay down this career, but I asked Him to please see me and allow my desire to become a reality one day. I thought the second opportunity a year later was my "one day," but then it was gone. As the months and then years went by, still with no path back into the world of radio, I noticed a change. I didn't desire that career as much. When we begin to desire what God wants for us more than what we want for ourselves, our desires begin to change. As I longed to get back into radio, I began to reflect on why that desire was so intense. Was I desiring this job to find my identity? Was I desiring this job to complete me as a person? Was I desiring this job to prove that I had worth? The answer in the early days was a most definite yes. But by the grace of God, He began to change my heart, and this desire decreased to an appropriate size in my life.

> When we begin to desire what God wants for us more than what we want for ourselves, our desires begin to change.

But before that change, it had been all-consuming. All I could think about was God giving me whatever I wanted, whenever I wanted. God doesn't work that way, and there's no joy in following Him that way. As I leaned into God more and more, I found that I still had the desire, but it was no longer all-consuming. I stopped basing my faith in God on Him granting me this desire. And incredibly,

I didn't feel any less loved by Him because this desire wasn't coming true for me. When we have the right response to our desires, we can get it together—even when those same desires are unmet.

The heart of every good desire is a deeper desire that can only ever be met by God. Dr. Curt Thompson calls this deeper desire "a longing to be known."[1] We long for that connection, that identity, and that purpose in life that can only be found in one place. The great news for believers is that we already have it! Our Father knows us fully and deeply. He knows our desires, and He wants our whole hearts. He knows everything, and He's asking us to give Him everything.

The heart of every good desire is a deeper desire that can only ever be met by God.

As we seek to have the right responses to our desires, we look to Jesus, who always responded rightly. When Jesus was hours away from being crucified, He prayed, "My Father, if it be possible, let this cup pass from me" (Matthew 26:39). Jesus brought this desire to His Father—a request for the cup to pass from Him. Jesus knew His future—He'd been in on the plan from the beginning—and still, He brought this ask to His Father, and followed it with, "nevertheless, not as I will, but as you will." Jesus presented His desire and then declared what was ultimate in His life—the will of His Father.

Jesus prayed a second time to God: "My Father, if this cannot pass unless I drink it, your will be done" (Matthew 26:42). Scripture says He prayed this prayer three times before He walked out of the garden and into His accuser's trap. Jesus, fully God and fully human, presented His desires to God. And when His Father told Him no, Jesus continued to do His Father's will, loving God and loving others all the way to the cross. The right response to our desires is to present them to God and then continue to do His will, regardless of whether they're met—not because what we want doesn't matter or because what we want is bad, but because our desires are not ultimate. He is.

As we chase holiness and yearn to act, talk, look, and be more like Jesus, here are three actions to take with our desires.

DESIRE GOD MORE THAN ANYTHING

When Jesus prayed in the garden, His desire not to endure the brutal death and separation from God He was about to face was real. He was not pretending to ask so that He could look more human to us. He *was* human, and His impending bodily torture and soul-wrenching separation were so real that He sweated blood (Luke 22:44). Even so, He desired God's plan more than His own. Jesus knew what was at stake—He was paying for the sins of the world with His own life. And He knew that this plan was better and perfect. Jesus is "the founder and perfecter of our faith, who for the joy that was set before him endured the cross, despising the shame, and is seated at the right hand of the throne of God" (Hebrews 12:2).

When you want more of God and less of you—more of God's plan and less of your own plan—this is the right response to your desires and to all areas of your reality. David Platt says, "Radical obedience to Christ is

> When you want more of God and less of you—more of God's plan and less of your own plan—this is the right response to your desires and to all areas of your reality.

not easy.... It's not comfort, not health, not wealth, and not prosperity in this world. Radical obedience to Christ risks losing all these things. But in the end, such risk finds its reward in Christ. And he is more than enough for us."[2] Radically following Jesus means that we, too, want to say "Not my will, but Yours" to our Father.

DELIGHT IN GOD

In order for us to desire God more than the fulfillment of our own desires, we need to delight in God. When you delight in something, you're a fan of it, you admire it, or you want more of it. When you delight in God, you admire Him, express your gratitude to Him, and long to be with Him. You admire God in all His glory.

The first time I walked into La Sagrada Familia in Barcelona, Spain, I was in awe. The majestic architecture almost takes your breath away. Construction of this church began in 1882, and as of today, it's still not done. And yet tourists and churchgoers line up daily to experience its beauty. As I stood there, taking in all the man-made splendor, I thought about how nothing compares to the beauty of God. Nothing. No chapel, no architecture, nothing. God deserves *all* our delight.

TRUST THAT HE IS WORKING ALL THINGS ACCORDING TO HIS PLANS

Desiring God more than anything and delighting in Him leads us to trust Him more. He changes us because when we are connected to Him, we begin to trust Him more. Philippians 2:13 says, "It is God who works in you, both to will and to work for his good pleasure." God is working in us, and we are working to do His will for His good pleasure. We trust Him as He works. It's a beautiful picture of us allowing Him to be our ultimate desire.

As we come to God with open hands, containing all our good desires, we can be confident, as my friend Tara-Leigh often says, that He is "where the joy is."[3] He's not holding out on us. He's working all things for good for those who love Him (Romans 8:28). The good news here is that when we delight in God and desire Him more than anything else, He gives us the desires of our hearts (Psalm 37:4). This does not mean that God grants us everything we desire. Remember, He's not a genie. This is saying that He *gives* us desires. He creates desires in our hearts that are from Him. Our desires change to what He wants us to desire. We desire Him first over anything else, and all of our desires take second place in order to know and love God more. The good desires become second to the ultimate desire. He will give us new desires for our hearts—*His* desires.

———————

Those great things we desire—motherhood, marriage, financial security, reconciliation, a degree, a steady job, owning your own business—they become second. They don't become invisible. They don't become unimportant. But they do take a back seat to the ultimate desire of knowing and loving God more.

As I think about personal desires being laid down for the desires that God gives us, I can't help but think about Mary, the mother of our Savior, Jesus. I'm going to do some guesswork here, but since I was once a teenage girl, these feel like probable or likely guesses about Mary, though they're not found in Scripture. Mary had her whole future ahead of her. She was young. She was engaged. She had desires and longings for her future. And then everything changed. She discovered that she was carrying *the Son of God*, but hardly anyone else knew, and in that culture, Joseph had every right to charge her with adultery, and her punishment would have been death.[4]

When the angel of the Lord told Mary about this plan to bring the Son of God into the world, Mary asked a very legit question: "How will this be, since I am a virgin?" (Luke 1:34). I wonder if she also wondered, *Are you also going to tell this to Joseph? Because this sounds crazy. What about the plans to get married? Now what? Will people believe me? Will Joseph leave me? What will people think about me?* The angel's response is that "nothing will be impossible with God" (v. 37).

Mary surely had desires for her life. She had plans and dreams, and even so, she responded, "Let it be to me according to your word" (v. 38). Mary's desire was now what God desired. She desired God more than anything and delighted in Him, so even when she was faced with unmet desires and an uncertain future, she trusted that God was working all things according to His plans.

May we all learn to respond to our desires as Mary did.

PONDER YOUR DESIRES

Pray

Father, You are aware of my desires—the good and the bad. The one thing I want to desire above all else is You. Would You please turn my eyes and affections toward You as my ultimate desire? Please help me see that what my heart needs most is You. Thank You for sending Jesus to be my example in so many things, even

in the way He laid down His own desires to follow Your perfect will.
Father, please make me look more like Your Son. Amen.

Reflect

How hard was it to identify your desires?

_____

_____

_____

_____

What desires in your life have become all-consuming? Did you
make deals with God in any of those situations?

_____

_____

_____

_____

As you look deeper into your good desires, what do you see as the
root desire that only God can meet?

_____

_____

_____

_____

_____

What desires do you think Jesus has for you? How does Jesus respond to you when you desire something more than Him?

_____

_____

_____

_____

CHAPTER 8

I EXPECTED BETTER

PONDER YOUR EXPECTATIONS

My husband, Aaron, and I are currently parenting four teenagers, so I feel like I have the authority to say what I'm about to say because I'm living this *every* day of my life right now: teenagers think they know everything they need to know about everything.

Now, before you think I'm dissing my teenagers, I need you to know that I'm dissing every teenager who has ever existed—past, present, and future—and that includes you and me. But seriously, it's as if a switch is flipped in our brains when we turn thirteen, and for the next seven years, we believe we have arrived and know all there is to know about life. We can't help it. Our teenage brains are convinced that this is the peak of life and that we have the key to all knowledge!

I'm way past this teenage stage, and probably most of you reading this book are as well. Those of us who are past it know that real learning begins well after those teenage years. In fact, I would go out on a limb and say that with each post-teenage decade of my life,

I have gained more knowledge—but I'm also leaving each decade with more questions than when I started it.

That's how life works, I guess. As soon as we think we have something figured out, life shows us how little we actually know. It's almost a cruel joke that life plays on us. I'm in my midforties, and I think the biggest lesson I've learned in this decade is this:

1. I don't know as much as I thought I did;
2. life is more nuanced than I ever could have imagined;
3. God is looking for humility, kindness, and empathy from His people;
4. and we have to stop expecting perfection from ourselves and everyone around us.

Expectations are sneaky, confusing, and dangerous. They are beliefs that something will happen or should be a certain way. They're sneaky because you don't always realize that you have them. And when your expectations aren't met, you can feel deeply disappointed, confused, angry, or hurt.

Expectations are tricky.

Sometimes we think a task is a responsibility—something we *have* to do or be—but so many times, it's actually just something we believe we *should* do or be. We put an expectation on ourselves that no one else had for us. It can be hard to tell the difference, and they're dangerous—especially when they're unrealistic, and so often they are.

Realistic expectations are actually responsibilities or obligations. I'm expected to take care of my kids. This is my responsibility. I'm expected to take my daughter to breakfast on Fridays because I told her I would. It's my obligation. My unrealistic expectation would be that because I'm their mom, I am expected to be at every single baseball game of their entire career. Because that is an unrealistic expectation, trying to live up to it would be exhausting and impossible. You could also have an expectation to look a certain way despite the realities of aging, be able to do more things than is possible in a given day, or be loved by everyone all the time. The most unrealistic expectation of all is perfection. You can identify the unrealistic expectations in your life by looking for things you *believe* you must do or things you think you *should* be or *should not* be doing. And those *shoulds* can be oh so dangerous.

THE NEXT RIGHT THING

I stumbled into owning a company over a decade ago. I didn't set out to be an entrepreneur or start something big; I just kept doing the next right thing in front of me, and the next thing I knew, I was a business owner. I'm fully aware that some of you have worked years of your life starting something, and my path has been completely different. No matter how smart you are, or how purposeful you were in creating a business, running a business is hard work.

I recently started feeling the pressure of owning a business and being the one in charge. I had people on my payroll, and that scared me. I put a ton of pressure on myself to succeed so that those who worked for me could continue to get paychecks and support their families. I understand that is my job as the owner, but this accidental business owner started getting uncomfortable.

I remedied this discomfort by expanding. I grew the company and added more employees. We added a new arm to our company. But as time went on, I began to feel an uncomfortableness in my life around work. I didn't love what I was doing, and more importantly, I kept feeling that Holy Spirit nudge that it wasn't what I was supposed to be doing.

For months, I wrestled with what my work life looked like. I wanted to quit and walk away, but I still loved the things I did—interviewing guests, asking good questions, writing books, speaking to women about Jesus. I began having an even deeper passion for those things. Although this new division was a great idea and adventure, it was not an adventure I wanted to be on anymore.

The only problem was that everywhere I went, people were so impressed with all that I was doing. I would walk into settings, and people would introduce me as someone who was doing so many amazing things. While I was honored and humbled, I also hated it. The amazing things they talked about weren't passions for me anymore, and I wanted to bail.

My wrestling lasted a few months, and to be honest, two things held me back: fear of hurting my employees, who were my friends; and the expectation that once you start something you need to finish it all the way to the end.

UNREALISTIC EXPECTATIONS

There have been many seasons in my life where I have gotten so frustrated with myself over not being where I thought I should be. I expect so much from myself, and when I don't meet those expectations, I suddenly feel like I'm spiraling. We expect to be further in life than we are, to be smarter about something, or not to screw up again. Sometimes when we fail to meet those expectations, we have a hard time recovering. And sometimes we wonder if we are still valuable and if God will still love and use us. We look around and think we're behind the rest of the world in something—knowledge, spiritual growth, our careers, taking care of our house, being a good wife—the list goes on and on. We put these expectations on ourselves. We make them up, and we enforce them.

There are also expectations put on us by others, like our family, friends, employers, and even our culture. And, as it turns out, sometimes we *think* the expectations come from others, but if no one ever stated that it was expected, was it ever really? For example, as I grew up in the church, although it was never explicitly stated, it was certainly implied that the best wives were the ones who stayed home and cared for their kids. So I thought this was what I was *supposed* to do.

I spent many years as a stay-at-home mom, and I've now spent many years working outside the home. Both were hard, and I struggled to get it together in both of those stages.[i] When I first started working outside of my home, I couldn't figure out how I was supposed to do all the things I believed I should be doing. How could I clean my house and work full-time? How could I be at every single school holiday party?[ii] It turned out that I put those expectations on myself—even though I thought the world was telling me to do them—and I ended up feeling exhausted and defeated.

If you find yourself anxious, frustrated, and unable to get it together from all the expectations that you put on yourself or that you feel the world, the church, your sorority sisters, your mom, or

---

i. I see value in both options and could never tell a woman what should be expected of her in her world. That's between her and her husband to decide.

ii. The number one thing I was happy to say goodbye to from our elementary school days was holiday parties. Why so many? Why do you need all the parents standing around the room watching the kids decorate cookies? Why? It was never my thing. Goodbye elementary school parties!

the PTA president are putting on you, I want you to know that you are not alone and that Jesus isn't putting those expectations on you. In fact, He's asking you to show up just as you are, even if you've failed yourself, those around you, or Him. Jesus is loving you and pursuing you no matter what . . . even when you do the unthinkable by defying all kinds of expectations you have for yourself.

UNNECESSARY EXPECTATIONS

In early 2014 I was invited to join a group of women to talk about race. At that time I had no public platform and had only just begun to consider issues that might be affecting my brothers and sisters of color around me. Three of my four children joined our family through adoption, and they are all Black. As a momma to Black children, it has never been lost on me that they would have to face challenges in their lives because of their skin color. I was aware that being Black in America was hard, but I didn't realize back then that they would be walking an uphill journey for most of their lives.

In this new group, I met the incredibly thoughtful and insightful Latasha Morrison.[iii] The same year I started in this group, twelve-year-old Tamir Rice was murdered walking to his neighborhood rec center with an airsoft gun in his hands. His life was taken way too soon, and as I stood consumed by the news, I kept thinking about my two Black nine-year-old boys who always played with toy guns inside and outside of our house. This shook me up like never before. I became determined not only to equip my boys for the prejudices they would be up against in life but also to never stop talking about

---

iii. Latasha went on to form her nonprofit, Be the Bridge, and authored a book by the same name. Please read it as soon as you can. I recommend this book all the time!

how, as Christians, we need to be willing to look our own prejudices in the face and repent of them.

A few years after I began to learn more about the racial divide and to change, I had a moment where I racially profiled a stranger. I had put in so much work with learning and listening, and I was parenting three Black children. I was immediately aware of what I had done, and it broke me down. I had been putting in so much work that I believed I was better than that. I should have been better than that—I was further along in my journey! I believed I had put to death any remnant of profiling or prejudices I might have had as a white woman.

How could I tell anyone about this moment? What would they think of me? I was a jerk. I was a hypocrite! Could this be the same Jamie Ivey who was actively engaged in conversations about race relationships, prejudices, and white privilege? There's no way!

While I wanted to keep this a secret, I did something that I'm confident was purely due to the Holy Spirit prompting me, because all I really wanted to do was hide. I called my friend Tasha—the same Tasha meeting with me in our Be the Bridge group. The same Tasha who had come on my podcast to have captivating conversations about healing our hearts from racial prejudices. That same Tasha who had graciously poured out some of her traumatic experiences as a Black woman to me over the past few years.

Although Tasha didn't answer my call, I still had the strength to leave a voicemail instead of hanging up. I shared the whole event as a voicemail and sobbed through it. I confessed to her how ugly my heart had been. I shared my disappointment for allowing an unmerited fear to overtake my body and mind. I apologized to her as a Black woman for what had just gone down in my heart, mind, and soul.

I've been ashamed of many things in my life, choices I've made, and things I've done. But this specific moment feels different to me because I was actively putting in the work to identify my weak spots. I was reading and learning and allowing myself to be changed from the inside out. I wasn't the same person I had been a few years earlier—so much growth had taken place. I had spent time confessing and repenting of injustices I knew I had been a part of and ways I had been compliant without realizing it.

EXPECTATIONS FOR MYSELF

A different shame overtakes us when we desire holiness and are moving toward looking more like Jesus daily. I wonder if addicts feel this immense shame when breaking a sober streak. I've felt this at other times, and perhaps you have too—this enormous wave of shame that crashes against your soul.

I surely thought I was beyond this sort of nonsense. It's this exact thinking that leads me to feeling like I will *never* get it together. Then I start to wonder why I thought I could get it together in the first place. I had an expectation for myself. And I failed big.

There was more work to be done. There is always more work to be done. My expectations for myself were that I would be further along in my journey than I was, and I felt like anyone watching would have expected the same of me. I had done so much work toward eliminating any prejudice that might be in me just from being a white woman in America, so failing this way stung massively.

The next time I talked with a friend about race, I felt at best like an inconsistent ally to my Black brothers and sisters and, at worst, like a fraud and hypocrite. I wondered if the words I was speaking were true. How could I seek justice for my brothers and sisters of color and also have had that moment—the moment that I didn't want anyone to know about?

My expectations for myself were, quite frankly, perfection. I thought since I was doing the work of listening and learning that I had arrived. The truth is that this work is never-ending, and my ability to learn from my mistakes, not only in my past but also in the present day, is proof of growth. The difficult part is that this expectation of "having arrived" and having it all together in this area of my life would always haunt me if I didn't adjust my expectations for myself. Not lower my standards, but honestly evaluate my journey.

Here's what we can't seem to remember when we fail to meet expectations: we are broken people on the road of pursuing Jesus for all the days of our lives. We have not yet arrived. We are not yet whole. We are followers of Jesus whose lives are marked with His goodness and faithfulness toward us. As I have seen in my life time and time again, our faithlessness doesn't change Jesus. But His faithfulness does change us.

Only one Person in the Scriptures has not experienced failure. Only one Person has never failed to meet the expectations He put on Himself. Only one Person has never failed big, like we do. Jesus never failed. And He alone is our healing in our failures.

We are broken people on the road of pursuing Jesus for all the days of our lives.

FAILING BIG

One of Jesus' disciples always makes me smile: Peter. I love Peter so much because he's so relatable. I see my teenagers in his confident, know-it-all responses to Jesus. I see all of us in his desire to follow Jesus and in his continued failures.

The night before Jesus' death, after the Last Supper with them, Jesus and His disciples headed out to the Mount of Olives, and Jesus continued teaching them as they walked. Then, Jesus said something that must have shocked the entire group—and specifically Peter. Jesus told all the disciples, "You will all fall away because of me, this night" (Matthew 26:31). I can't even imagine the tension in the group at this moment. They had to be thinking, *What the actual heck is happening?*

But then Peter spoke up. While we don't know exactly what the others were thinking or doing, we know what Peter was thinking and doing, because he said, "Though they all fall away because of you, I will never fall away" (v. 33). I like to picture him looking around at the others and expecting them to jump in with similar responses. Peter had an expectation that he was incapable of falling away from Jesus. He had only been at this disciple thing a few years, but he clearly expected perfection.

Jesus then looked at Peter and said, "Truly, I tell you, this very night, before the rooster crows, you will deny me three times" (v. 34). Can you even imagine how this must have felt to Peter? To the rest of the crew? These disciples had been walking with Jesus in His ministry. They'd witnessed miracles and seen lives transformed. And now they were hearing news they never could have believed to be true.

Peter didn't hold back: "Even if I must die with you, I will not deny you!" (v. 35). And all the other disciples said the same thing. Can you feel it? The devotion. The love. Peter refused to believe that he could deny his friend, his teacher, his Messiah whom he loved so deeply.

But Peter did deny Jesus three times before the rooster crowed. As I think about that night, and as someone who has also failed at the expectations I had for myself, I want to cry *with* and *for* Peter.

It is very clear that Peter didn't want to deny Jesus. He loved Jesus and proclaimed that he would rather die with Him than deny Him. And even when faced with Jesus' words of what was to come, Peter expected perfect faithfulness of himself.

All four gospels tell the story of Peter denying Jesus three times, and three gospels tell us that he went out and wept bitterly (Matthew 26:75; Mark 14:72; Luke 22:62). But the Gospel of Luke tells us a little more. As Peter was denying Jesus for the third time—literally still speaking the words—he heard the rooster crow. "The Lord turned and looked straight at Peter. Then Peter remembered the word the Lord had spoken to him" (Luke 22:61 NIV).

The unthinkable had happened. He had failed and failed big. How did he end up here? Only a few hours earlier, Peter had looked Jesus straight in the eyes and declared that he would rather die than deny Him, and now the Lord was looking on as Peter straight-up denied Him. What pain, sorrow, and shame must have overtaken Peter in that moment.

Thank goodness that "weeping may stay overnight, but there is joy in the morning" (Psalm 30:5 CSB).

IT'S ALWAYS LOVE

The next time we see Peter and Jesus interact, Peter is fishing. He's in his element and with his friends. It's not clear why Peter went back to fishing. Maybe he was discouraged. Maybe he was wondering how he would support his family now that the Messiah was dead. Maybe he just loved fishing, and it was a way to be with his friends and take his mind off of the last few horrible days.

When Peter realizes that it's his friend and Messiah, Jesus, on the shore, he jumps in the water and swims to Him. He doesn't wait for Jesus to invite him or call him over. He jumps. This is the Peter who said he would rather die than deny Jesus. We see the devotion. We see the love. We see the urgency to get back to Jesus.

Jesus came to meet Peter in his distress and prove to him that there was nothing he could do to push Jesus away. There's no expectation he could fail to meet—from himself or from anyone else—that could banish him from Jesus' presence. Nothing could separate Peter from the love of Jesus.

And friend, please lean in close when I say this: there is nothing that can separate *you* from the love of Jesus. There's no expectation you can fail to meet—from yourself or from anyone else—that could banish you from Jesus' presence. Paul reminded us of this in Romans when he said, "I am convinced that nothing can ever separate us from God's love. Neither death nor life, neither angels nor demons, neither our fears for today nor our worries about tomorrow—not even the powers of hell can separate us from God's love" (8:38 NLT). Whatever you have done in your life that brings you shame, condemnation, fear, or anger—whatever expectation you have failed to meet—it doesn't have the power to separate you from God and His love for you. If this isn't the best news for today, then nothing is!

Peter failed big, and Jesus came to him to make sure he knew that Jesus had not lost any hope in him. Peter failed big, and Jesus still used Peter to change the world with the gospel's good news. Jesus' reaction to Peter's greatest failure was love. He reminded Peter that He wasn't done with him and had great things in store for him. So know that even when you get it together and then inevitably fail to meet expectations, Jesus' response to you is the same as it was to Peter—love.

When I did the unthinkable and failed to meet an expectation I didn't even know I'd placed on myself, I felt like a failure and I was consumed by shame. I didn't have the right response to myself. I was trying so hard to love and understand my Black brothers and sisters well, and yet I failed. I failed because I'm human and everything is broken—including my brain, emotions, and reactions. How did Jesus respond to me in my failure? The same way He responded to Peter. Love. He forgave me when I asked Him to, He never left my side, and He's not ashamed of me. Moving forward, the right response for me to have for myself when expectations are not met—the response that overflows from a deep, intimate relationship with God—is love.

PONDER YOUR EXPECTATIONS

Pray

Jesus, You are consistently so faithful to us, even when we are unfaithful to You. I have placed so many unnecessary expectations on myself and allowed others to do the same, and yet Your expectations for me are all that matter. Thank You for loving me, pursuing me, and forgiving me when I fail others, myself, and You. Help me to reevaluate the expectations I take on, and remind me that I will be growing continually until I meet You. I will not arrive at any form of perfection while here on this earth. You are my perfection, and I will continue to chase You. Amen.

Reflect

Note: when it comes to inventorying your current reality, placing items in the expectations area can be very clarifying. You might initially label something an *expectation* (what you think you "should do") that turns out to be a desire (a "want to do"). There might be something you label as a *responsibility* (a "have to") that, upon further reflection, proves to be an expectation because you *believed* you had to do it. And when you are truly chasing holiness—to act, talk, look, and be more like Jesus—it gets easier to rid yourself of expectations other people have for you!

Think about a time when you failed to meet an expectation and failed big. How did you respond?

_____

_____

_____

_____

How can you respond to yourself with love the next time you fail to meet an expectation?

_____

_____

_____

_____

_____

Do you care more about the expectations you place on yourself or the expectations placed on you by others? Why do you think that is?

_____

_____

_____

_____

_____

What expectations do you think Jesus has for you? How does Jesus respond to you when you fail to meet those expectations?

_____

_____

_____

_____

CHAPTER 9

WHERE'S THE JOY?

PONDER YOUR RESPONSIBILITIES

In Texas, you're required to get your vehicle's emissions inspected each year before registering it with the state. This is not a new law; it's something I've been doing for almost two decades. But there have been a few years when, for whatever reason, my husband and I could not get our act together enough to get one of our cars inspected. The years just kept passing, and we still hadn't gotten the car inspected. And because it wasn't my personal car, I hardly ever thought about it.

That was until we gave this car to our new teen driver—and I thought about it all the time. I imagined him getting pulled over by the police, thrown in the back of their car in handcuffs, and hauled off to jail . . . all because his parents couldn't get it together. I know. Very dramatic. When my husband was driving this car, I didn't worry. He's a big boy and can take care of himself. But putting my new teen driver in the car, all I did was worry.

It might seem silly, but every time I saw that unregistered car in the driveway, it would cause me to worry for my son. Telling this story now, I'm keenly aware that it was *such* an easy fix. I experienced continual anxiety over something that could have been fixed any day of the week for several years. Finally, I took this car in to get inspected and registered, and as they replaced the 2016 sticker with the new 2021 sticker (yes, you read that right), I let out a deep sigh of relief, knowing this worry was now behind me. Fortunately, no one ended up in the back of a police vehicle, but this scenario still haunts me.

RESPONSIBILITIES VERSUS OBLIGATIONS

Getting our car inspected and registered is a responsibility—something Aaron and I have to do—because we are car owners in the state of Texas. When we neglect that responsibility, we bring unnecessary stress, worry, and anxiety into our lives. We all have roles—employee, parent, spouse, citizen, and so on—and roles have responsibilities. There are certain things you have to do because of who you are and the roles you have, and there's really no way around it. And when you get a new role, you get new responsibilities. The difference between obligations and responsibilities is that obligations are things you *should* do because you chose to say yes, and responsibilities are things you *have* to do because of who you are.

I remember when we were going through our wedding album for the first time. We were fresh in our newlywed bliss and probably enjoying a milkshake together as we looked at the photos.[i] I loved seeing the images of us on that day. All the planning and prepa-

---

i. We drank milkshakes almost nightly our first year of marriage. Oh, to have a twenty-three-year-old metabolism again!

ration were so evident. And as we turned the page, we both began to laugh. I had completely forgotten about this moment, but when I saw the picture, it came back to me. Right before my dad and I walked through the church doors to head down the aisle, the photographer captured the perfect photo of us.

I turned to my dad to thank him. I told him how much I appreciated him and loved him. And then I held out three of his credit cards. The instant my dad saw the credit cards, he burst out laughing, and the photographer snapped the photo. (I'm pretty sure I chose this exact moment so that our laughter would keep our tears to a minimum as he walked me down the aisle!)

Aaron looked up from the album and, half-joking and half-serious, asked, "Wait, why did you give those cards back to your dad?" I reminded him that our roles had changed. We were married now. And *we* were now responsible for our finances—not my dad!

THE WEIGHT OF RESPONSIBILITY

Responsibilities are an area of our reality that can feel so daunting to us, as they often affect other people and have big consequences when we neglect them. Circumstances and roles change, but God doesn't. He is always with us and for us. And when it comes to our responsibilities, God is more concerned with our hearts than our to-do lists.

Look back at the responsibilities you listed in your Reality Inventory. Is there anything you would add or remove? If so, revise your list so that it reflects your current responsibilities. It's possible that your list

Circumstances and roles change, but God doesn't.

didn't change at all. You can cross obligations off your to-do list, but that's less true of responsibilities. Many responsibilities are impossible to take off your plate, your calendar, your time, or your mind.

My role as a mom comes with many responsibilities. They weigh heavily not only on my heart, mind, and soul but also on my calendar. These responsibilities take up a lot of my time in my current season of life. I'm also a business owner. I've learned over the past few years that when you own a business, you have to adjust your calendar to reflect this. Lunch dates and midday workouts aren't as easy for me as they used to be. The fact is that our calendars so often reflect our roles and, thus, our many responsibilities. There are seasons in which our calendars are full of responsibilities and other seasons when they're less full. Seasons change, responsibilities change, and so do our calendars.

There are some seasons when our responsibilities seem to take over our realities. But responsibilities are only *one* area of six in our current realities. When the balance is off in our reality, we start to feel out of control. With other areas of our reality, we shift our focus, let go of some things, and downsize them, but this is often not true of our responsibilities. While we should definitely ask for help from our family and community in these times, there will be seasons when our responsibilities will be the largest area of our current reality.

When you move into a new role, you are inundated with new responsibilities, especially at the beginning. New moms are an example of this. You have so many responsibilities at first, especially as you figure out this new role. And if your baby is sick or has special needs, then there may be even more responsibilities. College freshmen and new employees also find that their responsibility areas are much larger than they had been before starting school or a new job.

And if God has entrusted you with many roles, this may be true for you as well.

Responsibilities are not only difficult to change or offload but they often affect other people and have big consequences when we neglect them. The consequence of not caring for your kids is having them removed from your home by the state. The consequence of not working hard at your job is unemployment. The consequence of not being a good student might be losing your scholarship, being put on academic probation, or not earning a degree. The consequence of not paying your taxes can be prison. There's a lot at stake. And we feel that pressure.

> **Responsibilities are not only difficult to change or offload but they often affect other people and have big consequences when we neglect them.**

When the balance is off between my responsibilities and other areas of my current reality, I often feel out of control and unable to get it together. Anxiety and worry enter, and I start to drop the ball. Something has to give. I have heard it said that we all have to decide which of the balls we're juggling are glass and which are plastic. We have to keep the glass ones in the air or they'll break, but we can let go of the plastic ones. They won't break, and they can be picked up at another time.

FULL PLATES

We know that getting it together means having the right response to our current reality, and that right response results from a rich relationship with God—so that's not a ball that can fall to the floor. In these responsibility-heavy seasons, letting go of many obligations usually restores a great deal of balance. Next, we want to make sure we've shared our desires with God and are choosing His plan over our wants, and we also want to ensure that we aren't striving to live up to expectations (our own or someone else's). And if we're actively hurting from something in our past or in our present, seasons of heavy responsibility might mean we need the help of a Christian counselor.

We will also feel out of control and unable to get it together when our responsibilities are not taking priority. As a college student trying to graduate and figure out how to be a new wife, I tried to add a bunch of obligations to my plate, but then my grades and relationship with my husband were negatively impacted. As a young mom who often tried to do more than she had the capacity for, I became overwhelmed and my kids suffered.

We're unable to get it together when we view our responsibilities as pain points to endure instead of blessings to steward. I have found that my responsibilities as a mother sometimes feel joyless.

> We're unable to get it together when we view our responsibilities as pain points to endure instead of blessings to steward.

Often, motherhood is like the movie *Groundhog Day*, where the same things happen over and over again, day after day, and I go through the motions with little joy and mostly discontentment. We can't get it together when we dread our responsibilities. Ann Voskamp says, "Being joyful isn't what makes you grateful . . . being grateful is what makes you joyful."[1] Lacking gratitude for the responsibilities that come with the roles

God has given you to steward will always lead to a joyless existence. When I look at my "Groundhog Day" and express gratitude to God for it, my circumstances stay the same, but my heart changes—and I'm able to have the right response to my responsibilities.

There was a time in my life when I was a young mom with two kids under two, and my husband traveled a lot for work. When I say a lot, I mean over two hundred days a year. Yes—*a lot!* I spent most of my days solo parenting, and on many of those days, I found joy and contentment. But on the days when I didn't find joy and contentment and I wasn't able to have the right response to my reality, I would remember a story that helped shift my perspective and realign my heart. I read somewhere that Billy Graham's wife, Ruth, who was also often solo parenting while her husband was engaged in ministry (and without our modern forms of communication!), would tell her kids, "Isn't it awesome that God chose *your* daddy to go tell the world about Jesus?" I can't help but imagine that the lens through which she viewed her solo-parent status shifted the moment her focus turned to gratitude rather than despair.

I have a hard time getting it together when my balance in my reality is off, when I'm ungrateful for what God has entrusted to me, and especially when I'm comparing my life to others'. We will never feel like we have it together when we're comparing our responsibilities to those of the people around us. It is often said that comparison is the thief of joy, and trying to find joy in your studies, your motherhood, your job, your relationships, your marriage, your roommates, or caring for your elderly parents when you are constantly comparing your responsibilities to those of others is impossible. We think we're comparing apples to apples, but the reality is more like apples to giraffes. Every mother is parenting under unique circumstances. Every student is learning under unique circumstances. Every

WHY CAN'T I GET IT TOGETHER?

We will never feel like we have it together when we're comparing our responsibilities to those of the people around us.

employee has unique circumstances in their life. Just because you have similar roles does not mean that you have similar responsibilities. The circumstances of your life and theirs are *not* the same.

Being content and joyful in this area takes work. Our brokenness and sin try to keep us from having the right response to our responsibilities. We must view our responsibilities through the lens of the gospel. When we have the right response—a gospel response—to our current realities, we are able to get it together no matter what our list of responsibilities looks like. Two truths from Scripture help me do this in my own life.

I am confident that God has not put me where I am on accident. Believing that God doesn't make mistakes when forming us in our mother's womb (Psalm 139:13) or in our callings on our lives (1 Peter 4:10), and that He has every day of our lives planned out, helps us rightly respond to our responsibilities from a place of trust, intimacy, and security. If it's true that every one of my days was written by my Father (Psalm 139:16), then I can trust that He didn't mess up when He created and formed me. The responsibilities I bear are fit for me in this particular season because God gave them, and I am not alone in them. My strength is from Him. My contentment is from Him. My joy is in and from Him!

In addition, Jesus tells me to come to Him when I'm weary. Responsibilities aren't always the fun or easy parts of life. Being responsible for your adult sibling with special needs is exhausting. Changing thirty-two thousand diapers for my kids was exhausting.[ii] Working a stressful job is exhausting. Working a non-stressful job is exhausting. Most of life's responsibilities are exhausting. But Jesus tells us that when we are weary, we can come to Him with our weariness. I find comfort in knowing that Jesus isn't offering us a plan to get it together by pulling ourselves up by our bootstraps and forcing it to happen. He's offering *Himself* to us. "Come to me, all who labor and are heavy laden, and I will give you rest" (Matthew 11:28). We all know that responsibilities often weigh heavily on us, and we have a kind, compassionate, and understanding Savior who invites us to come toward Him in our weariness. Jesus understands responsibilities.

JESUS AND HIS MOM

So often when we think of Jesus, we think of the big moments in His life, like how He turned water into wine (and became the wedding hero), or how He walked on water to get to His disciples. Maybe you think of how He treated others, like children or the "least of these," or how he told Zacchaeus to come down from the tree so He could eat dinner with him that night. I often think of how He treated women in a culture that didn't value them. And we all think about His death, burial, and resurrection (because they changed our lives and our eternity!). But do you ever find yourself thinking about Jesus' earthly responsibilities?

We think of His birth, the wise men showing up when He was around two, and how He got left behind in the temple at the age of twelve. And then we fast-forward eighteen years, and all of a sudden,

---

ii. Oh yes, I looked this up. An average child from birth to potty training will go through eight thousand diapers. I have four kids. There's your math!

He bursts onto the scene at age thirty to begin His ministry. What was happening during those unmentioned years? Alicia Britt Chole says, "Only three years, less than 10 percent, of Jesus' days are visible through the writings of the Bible. Over 90 percent of his earthly life is submerged in the unseen."[2] She calls those unseen years His "anonymous years."

Jesus had responsibilities in those unseen years. He was fully human, so He had roles, and roles give us responsibilities. We know that He lived within a family that had zero status or notoriety. He didn't come from royalty, so there was no option to lie around while servants waited on Him. He grew up in a regular, first-century Jewish home. He had responsibilities around the house and in His school, just like our children do today. We know He worked with His hands in either masonry or carpentry (Mark 6:3), so He had some sort of employment and financial responsibilities. Responsibilities are an area that Jesus can definitely relate to.

As we look to Jesus to show us what the right responses to our responsibilities look like, we see He prioritized one responsibility above them all: His relationship with His Father. Over and over in Scripture, we see Jesus make time to spend with God the Father. Time after time, we see Jesus get away to pray to His Father. He nurtured that relationship and knew His responsibility to His Father was greater than His responsibility to His earthly family, friends, or even His ministry. It's true that Jesus' relationship with God the Father is different than ours. Jesus is God, and He'd been in perfect community with God before putting on flesh and coming to earth. But the Son of God shows us by His example that as people with all sorts of responsibilities (and needs and desires and everything else!), the most important responsibility we have is as a child of God, and our most important relationship is with our heavenly Father.

I had a conversation on my podcast with my friend Jami where we discussed Mary as part of a series about the characters of Christmas.[3] As moms, we commiserated over what it would have been like to be the mother to the Savior of the world. Jami and I had both lost children at the grocery store and felt panicked the way Mary likely felt when she and Joseph lost young Jesus at the temple. But neither of us has endured watching one of our children die. My heart breaks imagining Mary at the foot of the cross, watching her son be tortured and humiliated as He hung on the cross for her sins. I want to weep for her and with her. We know Mary knew she was carrying the Savior of the world in her womb, because the angel told her (Luke 1:30–33). We can also assume that even as Jesus' mom, she couldn't have fully understood or comprehended what His death would involve, because Scripture says no one truly understood. And as she stood there watching her firstborn son die slowly and painfully, Jesus uttered some of His last words *for her.*

In His death, Jesus was taking care of His mom. Jesus' earthly dad had passed away, so as the oldest male, Jesus was responsible for His mother. Sure, He had other siblings, but at the time of His death, they weren't all sold on His plan for how He would redeem humanity. Jesus needed to make sure that His mother, a widow, would be taken care of. From the cross, Jesus said, "Woman, behold, your son!" as He looked at His mother, who was standing next to John, His friend and beloved disciple (John 19:26). Then Jesus looked to John and said, "Behold, your mother!" Scripture then says, "And from that hour the disciple took her to his own home" (v. 27). In Jesus' final, excruciating moments of life, He took seriously the responsibility to take care of His mother.

It makes me teary even thinking about it. What mom doesn't want her son to cherish her, take care of her, and look out for her?

Jesus was not only taking care of the cost of His mother's sins while hanging on the cross, but He was also taking care of her for the rest of her time on earth. Jesus' love and affection for His mom were evident enough on the cross, but He went the extra mile to take care of her in His greatest moment of pain and suffering.

> **Jesus is familiar with the nature and weight of responsibilities in this life, and He handled His earthly responsibilities with intentionality and purpose.**

Jesus is familiar with the nature and weight of responsibilities in this life, and He handled His earthly responsibilities with intentionality and purpose. He knew the most important thing He could do in life was to spend time with His Father, and His responses to all areas of His earthly reality overflowed from that deep, intimate relationship.

PONDER YOUR RESPONSIBILITIES

Pray

Father, You have not made a mistake with my life. I am right where I need to be, and I want to trust You with that. When I'm beginning to feel like my life is one big "Groundhog Day," will You help me see the purpose for my days? Thank You for putting me in the places where You want me. Thank You for loving me and helping me see my responsibilities through a new lens. May I constantly remember that You are more concerned with my heart than my to-do list.

Reflect

How do your current responsibilities push you to lean into God right now?

_____

_____

_____

_____

_____

What responsibilities do you resent in your current reality?

_____

_____

_____

_____

Ask God to help adjust your heart in your current season.

_____

_____

_____

PART III

SHAPING YOUR REALITY

CHAPTER 10

CHASING HOLINESS

Knowledge is power. Knowing as much as you can about something truly does give you power. We just finished six chapters together where we dug deep inside ourselves to find out what it is that sometimes makes us feel out of control.

This year, my husband and I developed a new and improved budget for our family of six. We didn't invent this budget, we just downloaded an app and got to work. The point of this budget is to list *every single dollar* that you spend, and then you will know where all your money goes. What we have seen over the past few months of trial and error is that even though I'm having to stop and think before I spend, I feel like I have so much more power over our money than I have in years.

Before having this budget, we just spent money whenever we wanted, saved sporadically, and then felt out of control when something unexpected came up, which is often, because that's how life works. What felt easier—to avoid a plan—actually made us feel more out of control with our money. Now when we sit down and take the extra time to figure out where every single dollar is going to go and account for every single dollar we spend, we feel in control of our money in the best way possible.

It doesn't mean we have more money, because neither one of us has gotten a raise recently. It doesn't mean unexpected things don't come up. It doesn't mean we aren't sometimes stressed about where the money for a car repair is going to come from. Things with money are still sometimes difficult and stressful, yet we feel in control of our money. It is no longer controlling us.

I have felt the same way as I have thought about these six areas of our lives we just talked about: past and present hurts, obligations, needs, desires, expectations, and responsibilities. Taking a deep dive into these areas of my life isn't like waving a magic wand over them and making them all perfect and better. I still have past and present hurts I'm walking through. I continue to take things to the Lord and work through them with counselors. There are still plenty of things I have obligated myself to with my yes that I need to follow through with. My bodily needs haven't gone away—my knees and back still need my attention. I'm constantly asking God if the desires I have are from Him, for Him, or all about myself. The unrealistic expectations I continue to put on myself have to be evaluated consistently and brought back into reality, and the responsibilities on my plate seem never to diminish; they just shift.

Acknowledging them and calling them out doesn't always change them, but it does give me perspective, grace for myself, and power over my life. I wish I could tell you that when you PONDER your current reality, everything will become manageable and good. I can't promise anything like that. But I can promise you that when you evaluate your current realities you can kick those unrealistic expectations to the curb and find relief in God's truth about yourself, His love for you, and discover what having it together truly means.

SET APART

As we take steps toward getting it all together, we first need to lay a foundation for something. The way we get it together is by having the right reactions to our current reality. Earlier in the book (chapter 2), we saw that everything has been broken since nearly the beginning of time. Now, what do we do with all that? We pursue holiness.

Holiness is a big church word with a very simple meaning: to be set apart. We are called to be holy, set apart for God.

For us to pursue holiness, a few things must happen. First, we need to be born again through the Spirit of God. There is a fundamental shift that happens when we follow Jesus. Paul said, "If anyone is in Christ, he is a new creation. The old has passed away; behold, the new has come" (2 Corinthians 5:17). When you decide you want to follow Jesus and trust Him as your Lord and Savior, you are a new person. That is good news!

> **We are called to be holy, set apart for God.**

Once we have this relationship with the Father, the Son, and the Spirit, we need to cultivate it—just as we would want to cultivate any relationship we might have. "Holiness is not an aspect of God; holy is who He is through and through."[1] There's no way to pursue holiness without pursuing God. It will never happen, because they go hand in hand. To know God is to know His Word. To know His Word is to know Jesus. To know Jesus is to have the Spirit. Through the Spirit, our will becomes His will and our desires become His desires. This is our path to pursuing holiness.

As we grow in our understanding of God and cultivate a friendship with Jesus and His Spirit, we will desire to sin less and pursue goodness. A desire to kill our weaknesses rises up in us. We see ways we have justified actions and behaviors, and our new hearts want to put those old things to death. A sure sign of growth in our faith is the desire to do what is right over the desire to do what we want. I wish this happened as soon as we started following Jesus and then we could be done with having to lay down our own desires in order to do what is right. This is a process that requires us to lay down our own desires time and time again.

I recently began watching a show I was so excited about. I had already watched the first season, and although it had some questionable content, I dove into the second season full of anticipation. I wasn't even ten minutes into the first episode when I felt that all-too-familiar nudge in my spirit telling me that this might not be the best show for me to spend my time on. There were already plotlines full of sexual immorality, infidelity, and an almost naked man. I could tell that God was protecting me by asking me not to partake of it. One of my best friends had already watched the show, and I couldn't wait to talk with her about it. I wanted to watch it so badly. Yet I knew I shouldn't.[i] I turned it off and told my husband about my decision (because this girl needs accountability!).

If I'm honest, I still *want* to watch this show. It pops up every time I open Hulu, practically begging me to finish that first episode. Yet pursuing God's will in my life is pushing me to desire to do what I know is right over what I want. As we chase holiness—yearning to act, talk, look, and be more like Jesus—we develop the right response to our realities.

---

i. This is not about what shows Christians should and shouldn't watch. Rather, it's about listening to the Holy Spirit and pursuing what He asks of you over what you want.

PRIORITIES

In 2020, there was an election in America. There was also a pandemic across the entire world. Add in an uprising about the injustice of racial inequality in America, and it was a doozy of a year. I felt so much frustration as I listened to politicians try to appeal to the evangelical voters in that election cycle.

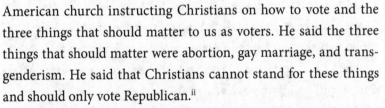

As we chase holiness— yearning to act, talk, look, and be more like Jesus— we develop the right response to our realities.

During this time, I was listening to the *Holy Post* podcast, which I listen to weekly. They started talking about an article written by a leader in the American church instructing Christians on how to vote and the three things that should matter to us as voters. He said the three things that should matter were abortion, gay marriage, and transgenderism. He said that Christians cannot stand for these things and should only vote Republican.[ii]

So often, people think these are the only topics that matter to Christians. As the podcast hosts discussed this, Skye Jethani explained that there are two competing versions of Christianity at work: "Cosmic Christianity" and "Crotch Christianity."[2]

Cosmic Christianity is a version where God cares about all things. Christ came to redeem all things, and He is bringing all things under submission to Him. This leads us, as followers of Jesus, to care about everything—throughout our vocations and society. Everything matters.

---

ii. I can think of a million more things that should matter greatly to us as citizens of this country and of a greater kingdom. I have big feelings about church leaders telling people how to vote. Isn't it illegal?!

Crotch Christianity proclaims that God only cares about what's happening in our crotches. In this version, sexuality, gay marriage, and abortion become the primary concerns. I know, crazy, right? I haven't stopped thinking about that since I first heard it explained. As I have thought about this idea of focusing so much on what happens between our legs, it got me thinking about my journey with faith.

When I was growing up in church, I understood that the way to be a "good Christian" was not to have sex until you were a married woman. It was the highest goal and sometimes felt like the only marker. The emphasis on waiting to have sex until marriage seeped into every conference, every weekend retreat, and every Sunday school class.

I don't remember anyone saying aloud that this was the standard of holiness for teenagers who wanted to be more like Jesus, but it sure felt like it. Every talk on purity was centered on what happened between our legs and not what was happening in our hearts. So when I was sixteen and had sex with my boyfriend for the first time, I quit trying to have any relationship with God altogether. I felt as though my chance to be with God was over. But isn't there so much more to following Jesus than sex? Doesn't He also care about how we treat those we interact with? Doesn't He also care about the gospel going to the ends of the earth? Doesn't He also care about the people living in poverty in our communities? Doesn't He also care about every person—no matter their skin color, income, sexual orientation, or gender—knowing they are loved and valued?

I'm not saying God doesn't care about our sexuality—He cares a lot! But it's not *all* He cares about. When we have a narrow view of holiness and elevate one aspect of our character above all others, I think we become like the Pharisees walking around trying to make everyone else feel bad. There are certain seasons in your life when focusing on one thing over another is needed. But declaring that one thing is the standard for all things? No, thank you.

Jesus made this abundantly clear in the book of Matthew when He said, "But I say to you that everyone who looks at a woman with lustful intent has already committed adultery with her in his heart" (5:28). He makes our sexuality way more than what happens between our legs. It's our hearts that He's after. And in case you didn't realize, what happens in your heart affects your entire body.

HOLISTIC HOLINESS

It seems like our current culture of being consumed with just a few things is leading us down a path of destruction.[iii] Jesus is after your whole heart and wants to change your whole life. Following Him and pursuing holiness, being set apart and different, will often make you feel dazed and confused in our North American Christian culture that often seems hyperfocused on only a few parameters for deciding what it looks like to follow God. You will feel as if you don't fit or belong anywhere. You will start to weep over what makes God weep and chase after things that move His heart toward justice and mercy. You will not find yourself aligning with any of our political parties. Chasing holiness will set you apart, changing you in ways you never expected and maybe never even thought possible.

Jesus is after your whole heart and wants to change your whole life.

---

iii. Of course, I'm speaking very broadly here, and my context is US Christian culture.

So often, we are chasing a version of getting it together that is not only unsustainable but unreachable. A version we created. A version those around us created. What we should be chasing is holiness. When we get those confused, we feel burned out and discouraged. Here are a few questions for you to wrestle with on your own. Feel free to pause, get out your journal, or write all over your book. (It's yours. You bought it! Unless you got it at the library—which, in that case, keep it clean.)

1. Am I more concerned about what people think about me or what God thinks about me?
2. Am I trying to do more *so that* God will love me or *because* God loves me?
3. Do I care for my body to impress people or because I desire to care for what God has given me?
4. Am I not dealing with my past because it just feels too hard to go back in time and address the feelings?

Holiness says, *I want to spend my days growing in my love, knowledge, and relationship with God.* But what we so often say is, *I want to feel and appear as though I have it all together.* Do you see the difference? One is internally focused, and the other is externally focused. One will bring you closer to God, and the other will leave you feeling stressed out and frazzled.

Over the past few years, I've been thinking about this idea of getting it together. As a working woman, I often feel discouraged when I am not where I'm "supposed to be" on my professional journey. I think I should have accomplished more, made more money, and earned more accolades. When I look at where I am compared to this made-up expectation, I feel discouraged.

When my kids were little, there was this moment when it was unbelievably evident that I was trying to look like a good mom rather than desiring to love my kids well. I don't remember what exactly was happening, but I'll never forget the feeling I had when my child confronted me with my desire to look good on the outside, no matter the cost.

We were probably at the mall or the park, because I spent so many hours there when my kids were little. I wasn't shopping for anything at the mall—just walking around with them strapped into the stroller. They got a treat, I got some steps in, and at the end of the mall was a playground. I could sit and relax (kind of) and let my kids run their little legs to Jell-O. One of my kids did something, and I corrected them in a domineering way. I wanted all the other moms to know that my kid would not get away with that. No way. But then, my kid looked straight at me and said, "You never tell me I can't do that at home!"

There it was. I couldn't argue with that. I never corrected that behavior at home because, let's be honest, I was probably tired or distracted, or it didn't seem like that big of a deal. But then, in public, I needed all the other parents to know that I knew what I was doing, that I had my kids under control, and that I would discipline them when they misbehaved.

The desire to have my kids under control led me to sacrifice a beautiful moment of freedom. If I truly didn't think what my child was doing was wrong, then my only reasoning for disciplining them was so that all the other moms would think I was a good mom. I wasn't loving like Jesus; instead, I wanted the opinions of other moms to be that I had it all together. I was simply seeking the approval of others, this made-up expectation, over seeking to do what was right in the eyes of God.

"Who would we be if God did not use the Spirit, use the church, and use the Word to tell us who we are really, so we can bring that to God and He can make us more like Himself?"[3] All of the ways God comes to us and reminds us we are different and need to pursue things above this earth are good for us (Colossians 3:2). It might be hard, it might be messy, and it might be uncomfortable. But it's good and right.

GETTING UNSTUCK

When Jackie Hill Perry came on my podcast, we talked about holiness because she'd written one of the best books in the last decade about holiness.[4] I asked her a question that so many of us are wondering: What does pursuing holiness do for us when, on this side of heaven, we are full of sin and will always fall short? I think this is where so many of us feel we can never get it together. We keep failing, and therefore we feel distant from God. We keep failing, and therefore we feel like we'll never be where we should be.

Her reply was something I have yet to forget: "What it [holiness] should not do for us is produce self-centered shame, which is, *I'm so aware of my imperfections that it's keeping me from moving. It's where I'm stuck in self-pity and awareness.*"[5] Her point is that when we realize we aren't where we should be, we look to Jesus, the founder and perfecter of our faith. He has started a good work in us and He will finish it. We will never be perfected this side of heaven, but that doesn't mean we should condemn ourselves and declare we'll never get ourselves together.

Your failure to meet the mark—your sin—is not the end of you. Your awareness of your shortcomings and desire to do what is right are evidence of your pursuit of holiness, and that, my friend, is how you actually get it together. Let's be people who continue to look toward Jesus, at the work He has done in us and the work He will continue to do in us. Our journey toward holiness is with the work of the Holy Spirit, and one day you and I will stand before the Father, and He will look upon us and see the blood of Jesus on us and declare us righteous (Jude 24). Knowing that, believing that, and chasing that is how you will get it together.

CHAPTER 11

ACKNOWLEDGE

YOU ARE NOT YOUR STRUGGLE

I love a good crime drama, and my kids do too. Recently they had some friends over, and they were talking about a new series about Jeffrey Dahmer, one of the most notorious serial killers in recent times. I hadn't seen the show, but my husband had, so he joined in the conversation while I just listened.

It wasn't long before one of the boys asked the elephant-in-the-room question—the one so many of them were wondering but only one dared to say aloud. "How could he claim to be a Christian and do the horrible things he did?"

We've probably all wondered that same thing before. It's the question we ask when we think of "those people" who have committed the worst crimes. A pastor in Wisconsin, Roy Ratcliff, befriended Jeffrey while he was in prison and met with him weekly after his conversion to Christianity (which happened while in prison). In his book *Dark Journey Deep Grace*, Ratcliff writes about this friendship and mentorship with Jeffrey. He shares that one of his church members once said, "If Jeffrey is going to heaven, then I don't want to be there."[1]

I wouldn't take my own feelings about Jeffrey and his salvation that far, but I'd be lying if I said I haven't wondered how someone like that could get into heaven. The boys who were gathered in my game room that day were asking the same questions. How does someone who murders people and does terrible things to others get into heaven? And then the bigger question: How does God let them in? And then even bigger: How could God *love* him?

When we talk about Jeffrey Dahmer, we talk about his crimes, defining him by his sin. He is a murderer. A pedophile. He did some of the worst things that any of us could ever imagine. Defining him by the grace of Jesus is never the first thing that pops into our minds—if it pops in there at all.

I know this example is extreme. But if we're honest, there are probably things in our own lives that we feel should disqualify us from eternity with God. And there are probably some things that we feel should disqualify us from His love right now while we are living on earth.

This is also difficult because we define people by their sins and struggles all the time. If you struggle with alcohol, you are defined as an alcoholic. If you struggle with food restriction, you are defined as someone with an eating disorder. If you failed classes in school and didn't graduate, you are a dropout. A mother who places her child for adoption is referred to as a birth mom—a constant reminder of that season. People define others by their actions all the time: She is a liar. He is a cheat. She is a gossip.

I want you to take a few minutes to examine your life and the ways that either you or others define you. Let's talk about *all* the things— the good *and* the bad. Do this here in the book or in your journal.

WHAT DEFINES ME?

List terms that someone might use to define you. This could include your roles, responsibilities, personality, job, hobbies, or sin struggles.

How did you feel writing it all out? Did it take a while to think about how you define yourself or how the world defines you? So often we are hardest on ourselves. The way we see ourselves is often so clouded with pain and shame. Here's my list:

What Defines Me?

Mom	Jealous	Enneagram 6
Wife	Christian	Angry
Podcaster	Daughter	Fearful
Friend	Teacher	Worrier
Dreamer	Vain	Anxiety-Driven
ENFJ	Procrastinator	Sexual Struggles
Author	Backslider	Nagger

Writing it all out and seeing how my sin and struggles can define me feels heavy. I believe we become the people we think we are. For example, I tend to be fear-driven. I think of every worst-case scenario you can imagine and work backward. What if the building is on fire? No worries! I've already figured out how to get us all out. What would I do if my kid tells me he got his girlfriend pregnant? No worries! I've already worked through those emotions. How would I react if a bomb goes off at a sporting event? It's okay! I've made a mental note of where all the exits are. You see my point.[i] It's easy for me to be driven by fear, which means I am often anxious, which leads me to define myself as an anxious person. And yet God doesn't put that label on me. The great news about God and His love for us is that He defines us by someone *else's* actions. Crazy, right?

The great news about God and His love for us is that He defines us by someone *else's* actions.

The good news for us Christians is that God loved us so much that He sent His Son, Jesus, to come to earth

---

i. You haven't even begun to see the number of worst-case scenarios I have worked through over my four decades of life!

and make a way for us to be united back to Him. Jesus made a way for us to be reconciled to God, and that reconciliation did so much for us—including giving us a new definition. Bryan Stevenson said, "Each of us is more than the worst thing we've ever done."[2] God says that as a follower of Jesus, you are no longer defined by your sin, struggle, or the worst thing you have ever done. The blood Jesus shed on the cross defines you.

The sacrifice Jesus made on our behalf *is* our new definition. Everything has changed now. You, my friend, are defined as a child of God, which cancels out all other definitions.

How scandalous it is to be defined as a child of God. How crazy it is that Jesus' sacrifice for us on the cross changes our whole identity! The struggles in your life may be true, but your struggle isn't *the* truth. You might feel like you're defined by your past, sins, and struggles, but they're just part of your story. What's truer than anything else in your life is that you are a child of God. God calls you His child. What else does He say about us?

He says we are *loved*. "For God so loved the world, that he gave his only Son, that whoever believes in him should not perish but have eternal life" (John 3:16).

> The struggles in your life may be true, but your struggle isn't *the* truth.

He says we are *chosen*. "But you are a chosen race, a royal priesthood, a holy nation, a people for his own possession, that you may proclaim the excellencies of him who called you out of darkness into his marvelous light" (1 Peter 2:9).

He says we are *forgiven*. "If we confess our sins, he is faithful and just to forgive us our sins and to cleanse us from all unrighteousness" (1 John 1:9).

He says we are *righteous*. "For our sake he made him to be sin who knew no sin, so that in him we might become the righteousness of God" (2 Corinthians 5:21).

He says we are *His*. "But to all who did receive him, who believed in his name, he gave the right to become children of God" (John 1:12).

This is why you and I—and even Jeffrey Dahmer—can be defined by something other than the things we say or do. Jesus changes our identity.

I revealed earlier that I'm someone who creates scenarios in her head that are terrible and will probably never happen—but I always want to be prepared. I call myself a realist, though others might define me as a pessimist. I just tend to see things for how they truly seem to be, and not how they could be. Sometimes it's a gift, though oftentimes it's a curse.[ii]

I recently spent about forty minutes talking to my bestie. We hadn't connected in a few days (yes, we talk almost every day), and we both had so much to catch each other up on. We're each parenting teens, so most of our time was spent discussing some hard things in our parenting journeys. I ended the conversation with, "Well, these jokers are sinners, and it's what they do best." I'm not trying to be negative—just honest. (See? Realist—not a pessimist!) And it's true. Humans are sinners. It's what we do best. We've struggled with this since Adam and Eve took that first bite of fruit in the garden of Eden way back in Genesis 3.

---

ii. But if you dream up something new and want to anticipate how it could fail or go wrong, I'm your girl. It sounds terrible, but believe it or not, it can be quite useful. I am not trying to be a Negative Nancy. I just truly don't want to be caught off guard by something. I don't want to be thinking that all is right with the world, only to find out it's not. Sure, I can be prone to worry and anxiety, but I've grown so much in my ability to fight those tendencies like crazy!

I wish with everything in me that when we dedicated our lives to following Jesus Christ, we would cease to be sinners. But that's just not how it is. The hope is that as we grow in maturity, our desire to sin decreases, and our desire to chase holiness increases. As Timothy Keller said, "The holier we are, the more we cry about our unholiness."[3]

You might be thinking of all the sin struggles you are experiencing right now. I have no way of knowing where you are in your faith journey. Perhaps you have some sins you have been living in and enjoying for years that you need to put to death. Maybe you realize the small sins you have been ignoring are creeping up on you, and you need to deal with them.

The hardest moments for me are when I become keenly aware of my sin, because my initial response is to declare myself "the worst person who has ever lived, and probably the only Christian who would do such a thing." I beat myself up and wonder how God could love me.[iii]

Yet I open my Bible and see a different response to sin. I draw so much comfort from the book of Romans, where Paul talked about becoming keenly aware of his own sin. I find so much hope in this because it reminds me that no one is so advanced in their walk with Jesus that they are no longer aware of their sin. No one is such a good Christian that they never struggle with sin. We are sinners, and we sin. (And if I'm a pessimist, then so is Paul!)

Paul said it like this: "For I do not understand my own actions. For I do not do what I want, but I do the very thing I hate" (Romans 7:15). I get this so deeply. I understand those moments of saying, "Jamie, get yourself together" when I stumble into an old habit I hate or repeat a sin I'm working to defeat. If we aren't careful, we

---

iii. I've told you a million times that I lean toward dramatic and worst-case scenarios, and if that statement doesn't prove that, then nothing does!

can fall back into the belief that our sins, the actions we hate, and our missteps are the things that define us.

Paul went on to say, "Now if I do what I do not want, it is no longer I who do it, but sin that dwells within me" (v. 20). This isn't a get-out-of-jail-free card or a moment of pointing the guilty finger at our sin and not taking responsibility for our actions. Instead, Paul was showing us that as followers of Jesus, we are new creations. Earlier in Romans, Paul reminded us that we have become slaves of God and been set free from sin (6:22), so sin has no hold on us and doesn't define us. Yet we know it's still there because we feel the brokenness of this world each day. It crouches around our hearts, minds, and souls, begging us to take hold of it.

Our identity has been transformed through the death of Jesus on the cross. We now walk in the newness of life. Timothy Keller said, "Although sin remains in me with a lot of strength, it no longer controls my personality and life. It can still lead us to disobey God, but now, sinful behavior goes against our deepest self-understanding. Even in defeat, the Christian has a change of consciousness: the 'I,' the *real* me, loves the law of God. Sin, on the other hand, is 'it.'"[4] As Christians, we love the law and want to do what is right. This is the change that took place in us when the Holy Spirit was given to us. Our sinful nature is still in us, but it doesn't get the final word.

Scripture tells us that people were given over to their sinful desires when they "exchanged the truth about God for a lie" (Romans 1:25). When we begin to believe the lies that the world and sin have something better to offer us than God, we will always follow our hearts. "We sin because we believe the lie that we are better off without God, that his rule is oppressive,

Our sinful nature is still in us, but it doesn't get the final word.

that we will be free without him, that sin offers more than God."[5] If we want to be faithful followers of Jesus, we need to reevaluate our view of God in order to put our sinful patterns to death.

When you find yourself lacking trust, desiring to be greedy, being slothful in your duties at work and home, or preferring any of the million other ways we can let our thoughts and desires take center stage to what is actually true about God, that's the time to dig deeper and find the lie that you might be believing. If you are working too much and neglecting your family, you might believe the lie that God won't sustain you. If you are seeking connection from one-night stands, you might believe the lie that intimacy can be found anywhere. If you are using harsh words with your children, you might believe the lie that God is harsh with you, and therefore you ought to be harsh with them. If you are jealous of your roommate's success, you might believe God doesn't see you.

Friend, as we look at our sinful nature, we can see that sin does not get the final word. Jesus does. Your sin doesn't define you. The blood of Jesus does. These verses encourage us "that temptation and conflict with sin, even some relapses into sin, are consistent with being a growing Christian."[6] It's a part of being human. As Jeanne Stevens says, "My past stories of destruction could become a present declaration that I was a human being, and I belonged to a human experience."[7] Our human experience—which includes sin—is about growing to look more and more like Jesus each day, and He was sinless. Our stories, struggles, and sins don't have to define us—they can *remind* us. They remind us that we're human.

> **Our stories, struggles, and sins don't have to define us—they can *remind* us. They remind us that we're human.**

WE ARE NOT CONDEMNED

"Okay, Jamie, are you saying that I will continue to sin until I die?" Yes, that's what I'm saying. I know it feels daunting to think that this is how we will live. But if you are a follower of Jesus, the rest of this chapter is full of exciting news. I'll spoil the ending: you aren't condemned, and you can overcome your sin!

Let's talk about condemnation, shall we? To condemn something is to say that it is very bad and to disapprove of it. We condemn things all the time. I would like to condemn deadlines and alarm clocks. Just kidding! But on a serious note, we condemn racism and sexism. We condemn rape and stealing. Most things that we condemn have consequences attached to them. There's no one reading this book who isn't aware of condemnation. We have felt it, and we have dealt it.

Yet Paul said in Romans 8:1, "There is therefore now no condemnation for those who are in Christ Jesus." No condemnation. The amazing thing about these words is that they follow Romans 7, where Paul talked about doing what he hated: sinning. I don't know about you, but when I read the words from Paul in Romans 7, I feel them deep in my core. I know what it feels like to have moments in life where I literally hate my sin and wonder why I do it. Paul said, "Wretched man that I am! Who will deliver me from this body of death?" (v. 24).

When I became a Christian in 1999, I had to put to death a lot of sexual sins. Not just having sex but desiring intimate connection with men to make me feel loved. Watching porn to satisfy sexual desires. All kinds of things. And I did. I stopped having sex with my boyfriend (which eventually led him to question our relationship). I didn't want to look at porn. I was putting it all to death.

Then I made the same mistake I had repeatedly made earlier in my life.[iv] I drank too much one night, which affected my ability to make good decisions, and I had sex with a guy. I felt terrible. I was this new creation, and here I was returning to my old ways, my old desires, my old sin patterns. A feeling of shame and condemnation overtook me. I repented and accepted and felt God's forgiveness in my life. But then I got pregnant. Suddenly, everything changed. There was about to be an outward consequence of my inward struggle. Growing up in the church, I often felt like there was an unwritten rule about getting pregnant out of wedlock: you were the worst kind of sinner. So there I was, a new believer who had completely changed so much in her life, and my onetime mistake was about to bring so much shame to my life. I was broken internally and before God.

But the most beautiful thing about those weeks in my life of struggling through those feelings of shame and condemnation is that I truly, 100 percent, without a doubt, had never felt more loved by God. All the shame and condemnation I was feeling was coming from *me*. I was creating lies about myself. I was disgusted with myself. I was shaming myself. God? Never. Not once.

I can't explain it other than I truly was a new creation who had sinned—because we do that really well—and God was true to His Word about me: "There is therefore now no condemnation for those who are in Christ Jesus" (Romans 8:1). What this means, my friend, is that my sin, guilt, and wrongdoings against a holy God (not to get pregnant, but to abuse something God designed to be between a husband and wife in marriage) were not punishable in His eyes. Had I carried that baby to term,[v] there would have been a consequence

iv. I tell this whole story in more depth in my book *If You Only Knew*.
v. I had a miscarriage early in my pregnancy.

(and, most definitely, a beautiful consequence!) but no punishment. No strikes against my record. There are no "three strikes, and you're out" with God.

The idea that God sent His Son, Jesus, as a sacrifice for my sins is something I can rationally wrap my mind around. I read it in the Scriptures, and by faith, I choose to believe it. But oftentimes, I don't quite understand how He doesn't condemn us. I think it's the wildest, most beautiful thing about our God.

As you think through this truth, take it a step further. It's not just that there's no condemnation for your past sins or your present sins—condemnation no longer exists *at all* for believers. "It is not waiting in the wings to come back and cloud our future!"[8] God is not going to show up one day with a list of your sins in His hand and condemn you. He always has and always will show up with grace, welcome, and love. It's the beauty of the gospel!

This truth should propel you to want to please God, not so that He will love you more (because that's impossible) but because of how much love He has already given you. I read a beautiful illustration of this from a twentieth-century preacher, D. Martyn Lloyd-Jones:

> The difference between an unbeliever sinning and a Christian sinning is the difference between a man transgressing the laws of . . . [the] State, and . . . a husband [who] has done something he should not do in his relationship with his wife. He is not breaking the law, he is wounding the heart of his wife. That is the difference. It is no longer a legal matter, it is a matter of personal relationship and . . . love. The man does not cease to be the husband [legally, in that instance]. Law does not come into the matter at all. . . . In a sense it is now something much worse than a legal condemnation. I would rather offend against

a law of the land objectively outside of me, than hurt someone whom I love. . . . [In that case] You have sinned, of course, but you have sinned against love. . . . [so] You may and you should feel ashamed, but you should not feel condemnation, because to do so is to put yourself back "under the law."[9]

Knowing that we are not condemned pushes us toward desiring to live a holy life, set apart, because of the great love we have from the Father.

WE CAN OVERCOME SIN

Overcoming sin feels like a promise that just can't be true, like if I were to say you will always be happy. Nice try. No way. I wish. Or someone saying, "I will always be here for you." That might feel true, but it can't be 100 percent true. Life happens. Things come up. So if overcoming sin seems like an oxymoron, what does it actually mean for us?

As we discussed earlier, our desire to be holy increases the more we walk with Jesus, and our desire to sin decreases. That is true, but how does this happen? Do we get better at making good choices, or are we too old to party and act crazy? I wish we just got too old to sin. That would be good news for those of us entering the second half of our lives. But it's not an age thing—it's a mind thing. Romans 8:5–6 says, "For those who live according to the flesh set their minds on the things of the flesh, but those who live according to the Spirit set their minds on the things of the Spirit. For to set the mind on the flesh is death, but to set the mind on the Spirit is life and peace." The way that we live according to the Spirit is by setting our minds on the things of the Spirit. It doesn't happen overnight, and it takes intentionality to do this.

Our tendency is to define ourselves by whatever is hard in our lives. Parenting is hard, so I must be a "bad mom." School is hard, so I must be a "bad student." I watched porn again, so I must be a "bad woman." I lied to my spouse again, so I must be a "liar." But the truth is that we are broken humans who make mistakes. We learn from our mistakes, we yearn to do better, we chase holiness, and we rest in the identity that God has given us—we are children of God. Chosen ones. Redeemed. Righteous. Standing on those identities is steady; anything else is always shaky.

CHAPTER 12

CONFESS

GATHER YOUR PEOPLE

I recently had the privilege of speaking to a few hundred college students at a discipleship conference. The students were there to see what God had for them as they started a new year learning about the family of God, discipleship within the church, and living on a mission. I have a big heart for college kids for three reasons. First, I was saved in college. It's such a pivotal point in the lives of young people, and I'm an example of a life changed while in college. Second, I am currently parenting four kids on their way to this season of life, so I love every resource and conference geared toward them. Third, I truly believe that eighteen- to twenty-six-year-olds are making a huge difference in the global church—and I'm here for this!

At the conference, I engaged in a late-night Q&A session,[i] and I noticed a surprising theme in my answers. No matter the question, *community* was part of my answer.

---

i. College ministry leaders, you have my full heart for all the late nights you sacrifice for our students! It took me four full days to recover from *one*!

Q: How do I read my Bible more?

A: Ask some friends to ask you about what you're reading every day.

Q: What does it look like to fight your sin?

A: Among other things, find some people to hold you accountable.

Q: How do I make sure I keep God at the center of my life, even when I'm chasing big dreams?

A: Find some friends to let into the deepest parts of your soul. Grant them permission to ask hard questions.

Every answer unexpectedly included the need to be in good community to obtain whatever they were looking for or abstain from whatever was holding them back. I guess I shouldn't be surprised, though. I have seen community work tremendously in my own personal walk with the Lord, and in every single stage of my life, community has been essential.[ii]

When I was a new mom and felt like I couldn't get it together, I met a woman who literally took care of my kids *and* me. She was stages ahead of me (her kids were in middle and high school), and she became not only a great friend but also a great mentor to me. I knew that no matter what I felt about motherhood, I could talk to my friend and she would encourage me and guide me.

In 2011, I linked arms with a new group of women who became a hope and encouragement lifeline, and for two years, we learned together. The group included new and old friends who spent time together learning, exhorting, extending grace, asking for grace, pointing each other to the truth, and developing deep friendships.

ii. I also think I have talked about community in every book I've ever written. I can't help it. It's so necessary!

What I learned from those friends is that "we can confess our sins to one another because there's no longer any need to hide. Grace sets us free."[1] I learned in this group valuable lessons that I have carried with me ever since. So often, when a friend confesses something to us, we're "perpetrating lies that lead to sinful desires," as Tim Chester says in his book *You Can Change*. He means that our friends bring their sinful desires to us, and we inadvertently agree with them by joining in or making them feel as if what they are saying, feeling, or doing isn't really *that* bad. He gives the example of a friend saying, "My boss made me mad today." And instead of asking whether their anger reflects thwarted or threatening sinful desires, we say, "He sounds terrible. I'd have done the same."[2]

My friends and I became disciplined in not joining in the moans and groans of humanity but instead asking questions to go deeper into the issue. Honestly, I hated it at first. I wanted them all to stay out of my business and agree that my husband was a jerk and that I was not at fault. Instead, they put away falsehood and spoke the truth with me (Ephesians 4:25).

A decade later, I was asked by another friend to join a Confessional Community. I learned that we wouldn't necessarily confess our sins to each other (although we do) but rather we would confess our stories to each other. It was in this setting that I muttered the "Will I always feel this way?" that I told you about earlier. These friends reassure me of truths I have a hard time believing in the moment. So much has changed about me and in me. I now believe that "an important part of how people change—not just their experiences, but also their brains—is through the process of telling their stories to an empathetic listener."[3] We do that month after month as we invite each other into our stories and make space for our feelings and our growth.

As I encouraged college students to dive into community that night, it reminded me of how thankful I am for the community God has graced me with. As someone who fears people bailing on her, letting her down, and hurting her, finding a few people (I literally mean a few) with whom I feel safe has been one of God's greatest gifts to me.

It's possible that some of you are reading this right now and rolling your eyes thinking either that it must be nice to have so many friends (false: I actually don't) or that you could never go this deep with anyone (false: you totally could). I think the decade we live in might be the hardest decade yet to develop a deep sense of community. If this is you today, please know you are not alone. The older I get, the more I feel the tension of wanting great friends and not knowing how or whether I have the time to develop them. I want to share the importance of community in getting it together, but in case you are still looking for your people or trying to deepen your relationships, let me share this first:

1. Look for people right where you are.

   There are people longing for deep connection all around you in your workspace, the gym you go to three times a week, your child's preschool, or wherever you spend the most time—*real* people who you can hug and look directly in the eyes. While online community has its place, you are not going to find this kind of vibrant, life-changing community on your phone.

2. Your church home is your greatest community.

   If you are not a member of a church, my number one piece of advice is to find a church you can call home. God created the church to be a place where we could grow together. In that church community, "it's not just godliness we model for one another but also growth and grace . . . as people see us struggling with sin and turning in faith to God."[4]

3. Be the friend you want to be.

It's super easy to spend your time yearning for friendships without having any desire to *be* a good friend to anyone. If you find yourself in a friendship slump, consider evaluating what kind of friend you are to those around you.

4. Be willing to go first.

Oftentimes we are afraid of opening up, so no one opens up, and the people you sit with at the lunch table, the office, or in class never really go past being acquaintances—because no one is willing to go first. It takes courage to open yourself up, and when you do, I want you to imagine me there giving you a massive hug and whispering in your ear, "You did it!"

5. Be willing to be rejected.

The hard part about being willing to go first is that sometimes you will get rejected. I wish your willingness to put yourself out there would instantly guarantee that everyone would love you, like you, and want to be your bestie. Sadly, I cannot. Know that it won't always work out, *but* you will never—and I mean never—find a friend if you don't put yourself out there.

And once you have your people, love them well. Give them the greatest gift they can receive in life: Jesus. We all need friends who "instead of trying to fix us, help us to fix our eyes more firmly on Jesus."[5] Every single time in my life I have felt out of control, and I just can't seem to get myself together, my community has helped me to get back on track. When you're spinning out of control, having friends who love you, care for you, bear your burdens, and remind you of who you are in Jesus is the best place you could land.

> When you're spinning out of control, having friends who love you, care for you, bear your burdens, and remind you of who you are in Jesus is the best place you could land.

I want my friends to tell me what is true. When I come to my community and I confess something to them—either a sin I'm struggling with or an emotion I'm not sure what to do with—I don't want them to shrug it off or tell me that it's okay. I want them to hold space for my emotions—the fears, the worry, the anxiety—because they matter. "Feelings (even the worst ones) aren't a sin, they're a signal. Feelings, even the best ones, aren't Scripture, they're a signal."[6] My feelings should 100 percent matter to my people, but I don't want it to stop there. I don't want them to let my emotions win, because there's something deeper than what we're feeling. There's truth under it all. I want them to point me to that truth. I want them to *gospel* me. I want them to tell me what is true about myself and what is true about God, no matter how I'm feeling or what I've done. To tell me that no matter what happens in my life—whether huge or seemingly harmless—God still loves me, I'm His child, there's no condemnation for me, and He is *for* me.

Tell each other the truth. Always in love.

We've talked about finding community, building community, and sharing truth in community. Now let's talk about getting it together with our community. There are often things in our lives

God is asking us to lay down that are so personal and intimate to us that we could journey through that process with Him and not include anyone else with us. Matters of the heart are so deeply personal that unless you invite someone into your heart, they will never know your struggle with jealousy, greed, and so on. I've had moments like this where I have told friends, "Hey, I just need to say this out loud so that it doesn't win the battle in my heart." I needed to get the thought/fight/battle/emotion out into the world where it could be heard/seen/held by someone other than just me.

It is difficult to have the right response to your circumstances when you're in a battle that no one else knows about. That's why Paul reminded us to "take no part in the unfruitful works of darkness, but instead expose them" (Ephesians 5:11). The Enemy would love nothing more than to have us keep our battles in the dark and to think we can handle everything on our own. There are numerous reasons we want to stay in the dark and hold our struggles

It is difficult to have the right response to your circumstances when you're in a battle that no one else knows about.

close to us. We might feel as though we are all alone or that surely no one will understand. We might feel embarrassed and think we shouldn't be struggling with this anymore. We might not want to be a burden to our friends, or, frankly, we might not believe we need community and think we are fully capable of doing life all on our own.

I remember two specific confessions in the past few months that I have had to say out loud to someone. Both were things I could have told no one. One was a sin done in private, and one was something

God was asking me to lay down. I knew the darkness would win if I didn't share. I have stayed in hundreds of hotels over the past decade, and never had I seen porn directly on a channel in the room. That night was different, and by the grace of God, I didn't stay there long. But I stayed way longer than I should have stayed. I felt dirty and gross. I wrote about this scenario in my journal:

> Why can't I get it together? Two decades of no battle—20+ years. I am so very discouraged this morning and upset with myself. I'm embarrassed about this, and I have to tell a friend. I have to be held accountable over the weekend. God, please forgive me. I failed, and I know it. Why did I do that? I am stronger/better than that. This is such a huge reminder that the battle is never over. The fight is never finished. I need accountability in all areas of my life.

I went on in my journal to write out Psalm 130.

> Out of the depths, I cry to you, O LORD! O Lord, hear my voice! Let your ears be attentive to the voice of my pleas for mercy! If you, O LORD, should mark iniquities, O Lord, who could stand? But with you there is forgiveness, that you may be feared. I wait for the LORD, my soul waits, and in his word I have hope; my soul waits for the Lord more than watchmen for the morning, more than watchmen for the morning. O Israel, hope in the LORD! For with the LORD there is steadfast love, and with him is plentiful redemption. And he will redeem Israel from all his iniquities.

I knew that if I was going to stay in this hotel one more night alone, I needed to confess my sins to a friend. I had confessed to God that morning, but I was staying another night.

Dietrich Bonhoeffer wrote, "Sin demands to have a man by himself. It withdraws him from the community. The more isolated a person is, the more destructive will be the power of sin over him, the more deeply he becomes involved in it, the more disastrous is his isolation."[7] I knew that for me to make it through the weekend, I needed to confess. I was meeting a friend for dinner that night. Not just any friend, but a friend I knew wouldn't judge me and would point me back to Jesus. As soon as we sat down, I blurted it all out. Embarrassed and grateful, my soul was comforted by just saying it out loud. It wasn't in the dark, there was light brought in, and I was not alone. I confessed as she pointed me to Jesus, and then I told her I needed her to ask me the next morning if I had watched anything I shouldn't.

I need accountability. It's what friends do for each other. It's what community is built for. God has graciously given us each other to help us as we journey through life.

My journal entry the next morning read,

God, I confessed to a friend. I had zero temptation last night. Zero. Praise You.

Even though I knew in my head that this friend would think no less of me, I'd be lying if I said I had zero hesitation in telling her. I worried about what she might think of me. But I know that secret sin is where the Enemy thrives. He would have loved nothing more than for my

God has graciously given us each other to help us as we journey through life.

shame to keep me in hiding. It would have been his best scenario. Instead, I knew my shame would be overcome with grace and love when I allowed God to use not only His Word and His Spirit to minister to me, but also His people. Having community in my life helps me have the right responses to my reality—even if it's an area of my reality I'm ashamed of.

In a second journal entry from that fall, I wrote,

Story's choir concert closed last night with "The Lord Bless You and Keep You," and tears filled my eyes— how do we get to sing this here in a "Christian" nation where following Jesus isn't actually that hard? I kept thinking about schools in Iran, where no one could sing this, and most girls can't even go to school. What am I doing with my life? I feel such tension. Am I giving my life away for the kingdom? In Luke 16:15 Jesus said to the Pharisees about money, "You are those who justify yourselves before men, but God knows your hearts." God, I want You to begin to reveal the insides of my heart to me. I know it'll hurt. Please do it anyways.

The next day I wrote in my journal:

Botox, nails, lashes, clothes, are these necessary? How am I stewarding my money?

I remember writing this all down and feeling the urge to tear out the pages and act like it didn't happen. You see, I *love* all those things, and in and of themselves, nothing is wrong with any of them. God was wrecking my heart about money. God was wrecking my heart about entitlement, and honestly, He still is and might be for-ever, because I tend to be a slow learner! Two days later, I told Aaron I wanted to talk to him about something, and I poured all this out to him. I then shared it with some friends. Putting it on paper in a journal and talking to God about it was fabulous and much needed for my growth. Allowing another faithful follower of Jesus to carry burdens with me and tell me the truth about God's love for me and asking them to hold me accountable and help me to have the right responses were what I needed in both of these scenarios.

Community is essential to a rich relationship with God and to having right responses to your current reality. It's so hard to get it together without friends to support you, hold you accountable, and remind you of the truth. Community plays into all six areas of your reality. I'd like to take some time to go through each of the six areas and share examples from my life to give you an idea of how confession plays out in community. Remember, our life seasons and circumstances make our realities very different, but regardless of the differences between your life and mine, community impacts every area of our realities.

PONDER

P–PAST AND PRESENT HURTS

I've shared already about how often I have brought my past hurts to my community and how they have encouraged me. The last few years of my life have been some of the hardest I've ever walked through. In the midst of the pandemic, I had the hardest years of my marriage and some of the hardest years of my parenting. I have very vivid memories of walking laps around my yard while sharing some of my deepest hurts in real time on the phone with some of my girlfriends. The way they held space for my feelings allowed me to be real, and their never-sugarcoated responses were such great gifts.

O—OBLIGATIONS

When I don't want to follow through with a commitment, I look for someone to tell me I don't have to. I want them to agree that I'm a big girl and can do whatever I want, even if that means bailing on something I previously said yes to. I need my community to do two important things here. First, I need them to help me decide if I'm obligating myself to people, places, or things because I think I should or because I truly need to.

Second, I need them to help me see the importance of following through with my commitments and obligations because they know that deep down, I want my yes to be yes (Matthew 5:37). I need them to help me see that faithfulness in what I've committed to matters in this world, even when I don't feel like it matters. For example, I'm doing Whole 30 and Dry January right now. I said I would eat whole foods with ingredients I can pronounce and find in the grocery store and abstain from all alcohol for the month. And I really want to meet this goal! So I've asked my people to help me endure this month of no carbs, cheese, or wine by encouraging me to follow through with the things I said I would do.

N—NEEDS

I have a bad back. I definitely feel like a grandma when I say that, but it's true. Degenerative discs, protrusions, bulging discs— you know, all the fun stuff! The last time I had a bad experience with my back, I was at work all alone when, out of the blue, it went out. I found myself laid out on the floor, unable to move, and in a ton of pain. Thank goodness for modern technology! I called my friend Erika on my smartwatch and asked her to help me.[iii] Not only did she show up, but she showed up with her neighbor whom I had never met before and who happens to be a physical therapist. The two of them eventually got me up and onto the couch, and then we waited for Aaron to come pick me up. This feels like a silly example, but I felt safe enough to call Erika at a moment when I was super vulnerable and helpless—and being in pain is not pretty. That physical therapist friend of hers, whom I met from the floor that day, still checks up on me today.

D–DESIRES

In some faith communities, desires are bad and not okay to experience. In other faith communities, desires are just a wish away—if you are good enough and have enough faith. What I want from my community is for them to hold my desires with open hands alongside me. Not to declare them bad but also not to declare them the basis for my faith or the foundation of my faith. There are so many things I desire in this life, and I have zero clue if they are from the Lord or if He will fulfill them. I don't want my community to tell me I'll get whatever I ask for, and I don't want them to tell me my desires are dumb. I want a community full of dream defenders.[iv]

E–EXPECTATIONS

I shared a deeply personal story earlier in the book about the expectation I put on myself surrounding my journey to understand racial injustice in America. I told that story to only a handful of

---

iii. Technology for the win!
iv. My friend Jenn Jett Barrett spends her life teaching people how to be dream defenders. Check out https://jennjett.com.

people before writing it down, but not a single one of them responded, "It's okay that you reacted that way." Instead, they pointed me back to the grace of God over my life in moments of failure.

Often I find myself with unrealistic expectations, and that always leads me to feel overwhelmed and out of control. If I created a January goal that revolved around driving my daughter to school and picking her up daily, that would be an unrealistic expectation that would eventually leave me exhausted and defeated by day twelve. I love my daughter, but I also have a job and other commitments, and we have a great bus system in our school district. I know myself, and this expectation would become the determining factor of whether I'm a good mom or not. I'd be tempted to believe that all good moms drive their kids everywhere they need to be, never put them on a bus, and never rely on anyone else to transport them. If I shared this January goal of driving my daughter everywhere with my community, I would want them to ask questions and, through those questions, get to the heart of this unrealistic expectation. I could be struggling with my identity as a mom, I could be comparing myself to others, or I could be trying to prove something to myself or others—and none of that would be healthy. We need our people to help us identify those sneaky, confusing, and dangerous expectations.

R—RESPONSIBILITIES

We all have responsibilities in our lives, no matter what season we find ourselves in. I am responsible to my children, my husband, my coworkers, my county and country for taxes, and so many more things. In a few months, I plan on returning to school, and I'll be responsible to the organization for tuition, and I sure hope they hold me responsible for my grades! I can't always escape my responsibilities, but my community can help me prioritize them and have the right response to them.

I am for sure responsible to my children, but I desperately need my community to remind me that I am not responsible for their actions. As I'm parenting teenagers who seem to lose their entire sense of reason and brains, sometimes I'm left feeling as though my status as a mom depends on their actions. But really, my responsibility is to teach, love, and lead my kids—and what they do with their lives is theirs.

My outlook and perspectives are often formed through my community. I need my community to remind me of things that are true. I need my community to help me have the right responses to my current reality. My life today revolves around parenting, marriage, and work, but what is it for you? Revisit the PONDER part of the book, looking at each section through the lens of community. Ask yourself who your people are, how they love you, and if they continually point you back to the truth of Jesus and His love for us.

CHAPTER 13

ADJUST

THE ROLLER COASTER

I hate roller coasters. I remember a time in my life when I loved them. I also remember that during that time, I had zero responsibility for anyone but myself. Age and responsibility sometimes change your perspective on things. I remember the thrill I would get while heading up a steep incline, knowing I was about to go barreling down the other side at speeds only a racecar driver should experience. And so often, there was a thrilling new slope I didn't know was coming. Right when I thought it was all over, there on the horizon, another incline appeared—and I loved the rush it gave me!

The rush of the unknown is no longer a thrill for me, and the knowledge that I'm responsible for more people than just myself keeps me from getting on roller coasters these days.[i] When our lives are also full of tight turns, steep inclines, and deep valleys—when we survive one difficult season only to find ourselves plummeted

---

i. My bad back and bladder with a mind of its own are probably to blame too, but that's TMI for sure!

into another—a roller coaster is no longer a thrill or a diversion. The roller coaster is life.

Though your life is different from mine, all of our lives have ups and downs, successes and defeats, surprises and messes. What is true for all of us is that life is one continual, very bumpy roller coaster from birth to death. Our individual realities are vastly different, but the roller coaster is the same. And figuring out how to get it together helps us to buckle up, throw our hands up, and enjoy the ride.

I'm confident you already know this, and that is because you are

Figuring out how to get it together helps us to buckle up, throw our hands up, and enjoy the ride.

breathing. You are living, and anyone who has lived for more than a decade is fully aware of life's complexities. Pondering your current reality will look different throughout your lifetime. As your life stage, family, career, location, body, and responsibilities change, so will your reality. And as your reality changes, you may find yourself feeling like you're

back at square one of getting it together when you thought you had already made so much progress.

There are so many things in our lives that we have zero control over. Will you get the job you just interviewed for? Who knows?! I'm sure you are super qualified and showed up very prepared for the interview, but in the end, you don't have control over the outcome. Will your friend respond well and reciprocate your kindness? Who knows?! You can be kind and inclusive, but you don't have control over how others will react. Will your marriage be without major conflict this year? You can work hard on yourself, your relationship, and your communication, and you can serve your spouse well, but you don't know what difficulty the two of you might have to face together. Will you experience moments that trigger emotions you thought you had dealt with? For sure. You can work on those emotions, bring God into the journey, and develop mantras and prayers to defeat them, and yet you don't have full control over when those memories will arise. Will your baby be born healthy with no deformities or health issues? You can take care of your body and baby during pregnancy, and you will still have zero control over this.

We want to have control. We want to know what's coming. But we can't. We can't control the direction or speed of the roller coaster, but we *can* control where our eyes are fixed as we ride. We can fix our eyes on our good Father who goes before us, and we don't need to fear (Deuteronomy 31:8). We can fix our eyes on the God who leads us into righteousness and restores our souls (Psalm 23:3). We can fix our eyes on His truths, follow His Word, listen to the Spirit, and grab His hand and keep walking on together.

> We can't control the direction or speed of the roller coaster, but we *can* control where our eyes are fixed as we ride.

You now have a clearer picture of the six areas of your life that make up your reality and the knowledge that getting it together is having the right reactions to that reality. Hopefully, as you read, the Holy Spirit revealed some things in your reality that aren't working or need to change. Maybe you realized there are things you need to surrender and let go of and other things you need to pick up and add to your life. You may have uncovered areas of your life where you're not trusting God and realized how that affects your response to your current reality. The journey of getting it together is different for us all. And it is my prayer that the Holy Spirit has reminded you over and over again on this journey that you are a child of God, chosen to do good works that God has prepared for you (Ephesians 2:10), and that your worth is not tied up in your current reality. Your worth is set and will not change—even when your reality does.

This roller coaster of life keeps moving, and new joys and challenges come your way. Just when you feel like you've got the right response to your current reality, your reality may shift. So what do you do? There's no magical app you can download to have complete victory over your responses to your reality. "Resilience and victory aren't going to come with a swipe on your home screen."[1] We need to acknowledge and assess our current realities and also make a plan to continually reevaluate our realities as they change over time. Getting it together is a continual process. But just like any other process, the more you do it, the better you get—and the more you trust God and listen to His Spirit in the process!

> **Getting it together is a continual process. But just like any other process, the more you do it, the better you get.**

This continual process of getting it together not only looks different for every person but may look different every time you do it. When your reality shifts and changes, you can still get it together. Read God's Word and remember the truth about who you are and how much He loves you. PONDER your reality for a clear picture of what is happening in your life and how you're responding to it. Chase holiness rather than looking or feeling like you have it together. Bring in your community, lean on them, and respond to yourself as Jesus would. There's so much we can't control on this roller coaster, but we've learned in these pages that we *can* get it together. We *can* trust God and change how we respond to our reality. We can also take charge of the things within our control.

You can control your mindset. You can control your attitude. You can control what you add and delete from your calendar. You can control the times you rest and the times you run fast. The things we can control in our lives are often the things that help us persevere in the hard times and be humble in the good times. Think about that.

There are so many resources out there to help us take charge of our mindset, thoughts, and attitudes. Maybe taking ten deep, full breaths works for you, or you might need to close your eyes and count to ten. Plenty of smart people have developed helpful tools for us to access in these moments. But never forget that as a follower of Jesus, your greatest tool is the Holy Spirit. In these moments, pray and ask the Spirit to help your heart and mind realign to the truths of God's Word. You have access to the Father, and He wants all of your heart, mind, and soul—in both good times and hard times. I often have to tell myself what is true—even when I don't believe it. We talked about this. Gospel yourself. Remind yourself that God is not out to get you or harm you, even though what you are enduring might be hard. "O God and Heavenly Father, grant to us the serenity of mind to accept that which cannot be changed, courage to change that which can be changed, and wisdom to know the one from the other, through Jesus Christ our Lord, Amen."[2]

We live in a trying world, and as soon as we get out of one trouble, another one often shows up.[3] As soon as we are able to get it together, the roller coaster of life goes through an unexpected loop. It would be so beautiful if all our realities lined up with our life plans, but often they don't. Just when you get to the bottom of the hill, start to coast, and think everything is fine, here comes another steep incline.

My dear friends, do not lose hope. You are not defined by your roller coaster. Remember that the roller coaster is life, but it doesn't *define* your life. You have a toolbox with you on the roller coaster, so use it!

1. Speak the truth.

   The first item in your toolbox is honesty. Be honest with yourself about your current reality. Acknowledge when things are hard, and don't make excuses for your behavior. Look deep inside of yourself and let the truth come up. The truth can hurt, and when it does, our instinct is to hide it. But if you aren't honest with yourself, it's hard to be honest with others. When you are overwhelmed with something in life and it's causing you to feel out of control, ask yourself the hard questions. PONDER your reality.

2. Dream a different reality.

   When I'm feeling out of control, I try to dream and imagine things differently. (This isn't the place where I tell you to "manifest your destiny." I wish you had that power, but once again, the future is out of your control.) In hard times, one tool is to imagine how your choices and actions affect the way you relate to your reality. For example, if you continually feel overwhelmed each December at the thought of sending out Christmas cards, you might need to take this expectation off yourself. By imagining the time you would gain back and the stress you could let go of, you might decide to change your reality next December.[ii] Dreaming about a whole new reality for yourself can lead to discontentment,

---

ii. Wait. This sounds really good. I might need to take my own advice here!

jealousy, anger, loneliness, and isolation, just for starters. Dreaming of different ways to *respond* to your reality can lead to contentment, joy, happiness, and a whole lot of stress lifted off your shoulders. It doesn't change your circumstances, but it changes the way you view them.

3. Practice self-control.

You might think you have zero self-control, but that's not true. Let's not sell ourselves or the Holy Spirit short! You have been given a spirit of love, joy, peace, patience, kindness, goodness, faithfulness, gentleness, and self-control (Galatians 5:22–23). You aren't waiting on some magic potion to rain down from heaven—the power is already in you! Proverbs 25:28 says that "a man without self-control is like a city broken into and left without walls." Use the self-control that you have. Oftentimes I need to practice self-control, so I limit things I can have in order to build that muscle. It's not out of legalism but is a way for me to lean on the Father and use the gift He has given of self-control.

4. Trust the Spirit.

And if I haven't said this enough, if you are a follower of Jesus, you have the greatest tool needed and the one tool that makes all the other tools possible—the Holy Spirit. God has given you this Helper, Teacher, and Advocate so that you are not alone on this roller coaster of life. Imagine the Spirit in the seat next to you—never leaving you, holding your hand, and being your constant companion around every turn and incline you might encounter.

Friend, my prayer for you throughout this entire book has been that you wouldn't look for Jamie Ivey to help solve any of your problems. I want this book to be a resource of reflection for you. To dig deep inside and see where you need to give yourself more grace, where you need to apply more truth to your situation, where you need to adjust your calendar and expectations, all while leaning closer and closer to the Father and His never-ending love for you.

The roller coaster never ends, but your experience and attitude toward the ride are always changing.

PART IV

CELEBRATING YOUR FUTURE REALITY

CHAPTER 14

GOD IS ON YOUR TEAM

Watching little kids play soccer is the cutest thing in the world. Soccer is the universal little kid sport. I mean, who didn't play soccer as a child? Turns out—my own husband! He never played soccer, and I feel like he missed out on a lot of four-year-old fun. But more than that, his parents didn't experience the fun of watching little kids play soccer. And one of the greatest joys they missed out on was watching their little kid score on the wrong goal!

It never fails. Almost every little kid soccer game has one enthusiastic player who gets really excited as they kick the ball down the field . . . in the *wrong* direction. The field is wide open. There's no one between them and the goal—except for maybe their own teammate, who is waving their arms wildly and yelling at them as they score for the other team. But no one gets too angry. It is a path of growth for us all.

Maybe you did this. I'm certain that I did, and so did my kids! Usually, the parents and coaches chuckle. I mean, they are kids, after all. But if the child were to keep scoring on the wrong goal as they got older, we might want to rethink things. It's cute when it's little kids. But as we get older and play more competitively, our teammates might begin to question our loyalty. They would wonder if we actually wanted the other team to score or whose team we were really on.

We often feel the same way about God. I've had times in life when I've wondered where He was. He didn't feel present, and I sometimes didn't think He was showing up in anyone's life around me either. In those moments, I've asked God, "Whose team are You on anyway?"

CONFIDENCE IN GOD'S PROVISION

When we were in the process of adopting two of our kids from Haiti, there were times I felt like God had abandoned all of us—those who were living here in America *and* my kids who were still living in Haiti. Nothing was going as I thought it was supposed to go. And the people who suffered the most were two kids without a permanent home or permanent mom and dad. I could take the suffering. I was an adult. I was strong. But my kids—this just wasn't fair for them. I wanted them home with me, and it felt like God had abandoned us all.

We were confident God had led us toward adoption. We had prayed and asked Him to open doors for us, and He had faithfully done that. We had wise counsel around us, encouraging us and praying with us. Fully believing that He had directed us to Haiti, we obediently put one foot in front of the other, always asking Him to light up our path. We trusted where He was leading us, even when we didn't understand or see clearly.

But when things started going south with the adoptions, I could think of only one person to blame: the Man Upstairs. He had led us on this path, and now He was making the path rocky and unsteady. That wasn't fair. I felt like He owed me something, because this was *His* idea. He owed me ease and zero struggles, like skipping toward our kids through a field of bluebonnets on a perfect Texas spring morning. But instead, it felt like a blazing hike through the Grand Canyon with no map, no water, and no guide.

I know I'm not alone here in these feelings of questioning God's provision for us. We often don't understand what He's doing or why, and we begin to wonder, *Does He truly care? Is He really good for me? Are we even on the same team?*

Recently I heard someone say, "I'm just so angry at God. I want to punch Him in the chest I'm so angry!" The women around her didn't skip a beat. One woman spoke up and said she respected her honesty about her emotions with God and added that she was confident God could take it.

For some of us, anger toward God feels wrong. For others, it feels like a space where we can truly let our anger out, because we know God is always on our team. That's the group I want to be in—the ones who can scream obscenities and mean words to God, knowing that He's not leaving or abandoning us. He's not turning His back or raising His voice to match ours. He's not ignoring our feelings nor letting them get the final word. I want to feel so confident that God is on my team and that He's able to hold my anger, fear, doubt, and loneliness in His perfectly steadfast hands.

Isn't this what we all want? To feel safe when we bring our raw emotions to God? I think this is one of the reasons we love the psalms so much. There are so many feelings behind these verses that we can see our own emotions in them. The intro to the book of Psalms in my Bible says that it is "a collection of over 150 poems that expresses a variety of emotions, including: love and adoration toward God, sorrow over sin, dependence on God in desperate circumstances, the battle of fear and trust, walking with God even when the way seems dark, thankfulness for God's care, devotion to the word of God, and confidence in the eventual triumph of God's purposes for the world."[1] So really, *all* of our emotions can be found in the songs of the psalms.

In the book of Psalms, we see David pour out his heart to God in admiration and frustration. We see him say in one breath, "O LORD, how many are my foes! Many are rising against me; many are saying of my soul, 'There is no salvation for him in God,'" and then follow that up with, "But you, O LORD, are a shield about me, my glory, and the lifter of my head" (Psalm 3:1–3). He's telling himself (and us) that God has been his protector in the past, and he's declaring that God *will* do it again in the future.

We often get stuck on "O LORD, how many are my foes!" and stop there. It is so easy to declare all the hardships and forget the goodness of God in our lives. There have been many catastrophes in our world, but the biggest one I've ever lived through (and probably will ever live through) was the COVID-19 pandemic in 2020. I found myself crying out to God, wondering when it would stop. The lives lost, the financial ruin, the loss of jobs and purpose for many people worldwide. And yet God was always present and never absent in the midst of that trial. God is still the God of whom we can proclaim as David did, "You are a shield about me, my glory, and the lifter of my head."

Recently some friends of ours texted us early on a Sunday morning to tell us they had taken their son to the emergency room because of a high fever. He had been dealing with some bladder pain for a few weeks, but with ibuprofen, it had been better. But on this morning the fever was worse, and they'd been admitted to the hospital after a scan showed something abnormal. We promised to pray. I sent some cookies to their hospital room and told them to update us after they spoke to the doctor.[i]

The doctor told my friend that he wasn't 100 percent sure what was going on, but there was a mass on their son's bladder that needed to be removed. There were two potential outcomes: one would be removal + life goes on, but the other would be removal + cancer diagnosis + a long, hard journey. They texted this report to us, we continued to pray, and then they buckled up for a few days of unknowns before their son's biopsy results were ready.

Finally, they got word that it wasn't the easy road but potentially the longer and scarier road of cancer. I texted my friends, "I'm certain this must feel even scarier, as it's your kid. Begging God for peace." And my friend texted back, "Thank you, friends. I'm sad, but there is peace in this room. God started preparing us this afternoon. We've been through this before, and I know God is faithful and here." You see, this wasn't my friend's first cancer scare. She had walked through cancer just two years earlier, and she beat it. Cancer had already wreaked havoc on their world. They could have understandably screamed out, "God, where are You?! I thought You were on our team!" Instead, my friend remembered the nearness of God during her own cancer journey, and she trusted that He would be with them on another.[ii]

In Psalm 13, the author (likely David) was lamenting over circumstances in his life. He was on the verge of despair and longing for God's comfort. Thousands of years after this was penned, I still

---

i. I can't make a meal, but I can always have cookies delivered.
ii. Praise God that in the end no cancer was found, and their son is healthy!

feel the same way toward God in certain seasons of my life, wondering if I have been forgotten and if God truly sees my pain.

> How long, O Lord? Will you forget me forever?
> How long will you hide your face from me?
> How long must I take counsel in my soul
> and have sorrow in my heart all the day?
> How long shall my enemy be exalted over me?
> Consider and answer me, O Lord my God;
> light up my eyes, lest I sleep the sleep of death,
> lest my enemy say, "I have prevailed over him,"
> lest my foes rejoice because I am shaken.
>
> (vv. 1–4)

Then the song takes a turn for the better. It's as if the writer begins to reaffirm his trust in God. This is where I want to be in my life. So often, I feel like everything is falling apart around me, I can't get myself together, and I wonder how much more I can take. But then I begin to lift my eyes up to God and remind myself of His goodness and faithfulness in my life. It's as if I, too, begin to sing these words:

> But I have trusted in your steadfast love;
> my heart shall rejoice in your salvation.
> I will sing to the Lord,
> because he has dealt bountifully with me.
>
> (vv. 5–6)

I bet money you can't read those last two lines without smiling like me. I feel my heart rejoicing in His goodness as I read them.

I remember how God loved me enough to send His Son for me. I think back at all the ways His nearness has been my comfort and His Word has been my guide.

I don't think asking whether God is still on your team is a bad thing. We are humans with real and raw emotions, so what better place for them than the space between you and God? My hope is that we won't stop declaring our woes to God *or* expressing our deep gratitude for His love toward us. Life is hard *and* God is good. They are both true.

But it's in these hardest moments that I often feel most out of control and the least able to get it together. I've experienced this as a mom, wife, friend, and business owner—I mean, truly, every aspect of my life.

> **My hope is that we won't stop declaring our woes to God *or* expressing our deep gratitude for His love toward us.**

My friend Tova Sido has had one of the hardest lives I have ever heard about. She has buried children, walked through a divorce, and adopted children internationally. When I interviewed her on my podcast, we talked about her life and her pain. She encouraged listeners to adjust their wording when talking about pain and suffering.[2] When discussing how often we ask why God has allowed something to happen in our lives, she said, "The question *why* is a waste. The question should be *when* and not why—*when* something happens, not *why* did something happen—instead of blaming God, rejecting God, or getting on your knees and asking why or how You could do this. At some point, everyone is going to go through something. *When* it comes, what will you allow Him to do with you?" I was struck by this statement. Tova doesn't say this flippantly. She has walked through hell. Burying babies is something I will never know, but she has stood over the graves of three of her children. Her faith and trust in God in times of trouble have been born out of so much pain, and her words helped me adjust my own feelings toward pain and hard times in life.

You see, the question of whether or not God is on our team is the wrong question to be asking. As followers of Jesus, we know with confidence that we will never be abandoned by God. He's the captain of our team and He's the best teammate. I have heard story after story on my podcast of believers walking through hard times, and in Scripture we see stories of God's people enduring hardships and walking in the unknowns—and never do we see that God has abandoned them.

> **As followers of Jesus, we know with confidence that we will never be abandoned by God. He's the captain of our team and He's the best teammate.**

One of my favorite songs right now is about how God joins us in our hardships. Its lyrics bring me so much comfort: "There's a grace when the heart is under fire, another way when the walls are closing in. And when I look at the space between where I used to be and this reckoning, I know I will never be alone. There was another in the fire standing next to me. There was another in the waters, holding back the seas. And should I ever need reminding of how I've been set free, there is a cross that bears the burden where another died for me."[3] We are not alone in our hardships. There is great comfort in knowing that God is always with His people, no matter what circumstances we might find ourselves in. Even when we can't see or feel Him, He is always with us.

There is a moment in the Gospel of John where Jesus' friends felt alone in their hardships too, and it's likely a few of them felt let down by God for a time. John chapter 11 tells us about the death of Lazarus. Let me set the stage: days before Jesus was captured, arrested, and sentenced to die, He got word that His friend Lazarus was ill. The sick man's sisters, Mary and Martha, wanted Jesus to come and heal Lazarus. "But when Jesus

> **We are not alone in our hardships. Even when we can't see or feel God, He is always with us.**

heard it he said, 'This illness does not lead to death. It is for the glory of God, so that the Son of God may be glorified through it'" (John 11:4).

We know now—because we have the whole of Scripture—that Lazarus eventually died, and Jesus raised him from the dead. But as it was happening, Mary and Martha anticipated Jesus would come and heal their brother. Jesus had been healing tons of people, and everyone knew He could, so there was no reason to think He wouldn't rush to His friend's side as he lay dying.

Except, Jesus didn't. In fact, Scripture tells us that Jesus waited *two more days* before going to see His friend. The journey could have been done in a day; it wasn't far away. Jesus surely could have gotten to His friend in time. But instead, Lazarus did indeed die.

As she heard that Jesus was on His way, Martha ran to meet Him and declared, "Lord, if you had been here, my brother would not have died" (v. 21). Most of us have also felt these same raw, real feelings. Basically, Martha asked, "Jesus, where are You in my hardships?" She knew Jesus could've solved this problem. I have felt this too. I've had times when I thought that my struggle, hardship, or situation would've been better if God had intervened. Like Martha, I'm left wondering where He is.

I'm always encouraged by Martha's honesty here. She didn't hold back, and she didn't sugarcoat her emotions. She said them straight into the face of Jesus—the Lord of lords and King of kings. But she was not the only one. Mary also ran out to meet Jesus. She threw herself at His feet and declared, "Lord, if you had been here, my brother would not have died" (v. 32). Sound familiar? Both sisters shared their raw emotions and their feelings of being let down by Jesus. Both sisters wondered where Jesus had been in their time of need.

In the story, Jesus was finally taken to where they had buried Lazarus, and it is there that we see Him weep over the entire situation—weeping for the sorrow His friends were enduring, weeping over the evil of the world. Weeping *with* His friends. There is no getting around the fact that Jesus, although He chose to stay where He was and for Lazarus to die, was deeply moved by the sorrow of His friends. Jesus knew all along He would raise Lazarus from the dead, just as He knew this miracle was the beginning of the end of His ministry and that His arrest and crucifixion were just around the corner. Still, Jesus *wept* with His friends over their sorrow and their pain. Jesus wept.

I don't know your pain. I don't know your circumstances. I don't know all the hardships that are causing you to feel out of control and unable to get it together. But the God of the universe does. He cares for you, and He loves you. In your pain, He is there. In your sorrow, He weeps with you. In your circumstances, He has not left you. And He never, ever will.

This truth is vital—it's vital for your relationship with your Savior and King, and it's vital for your ability to get it together and have the right response to your current reality. Your responses are a result of your relationship with God. When your relationship is deep and intimate, when your heart is saturated with the truth of who God is and what He has done, you respond to your reality from a place of truth, love, and security. You are God's child, He is with you, and you are loved no matter what—and responses to your reality, to the ups and the downs, reflect that truth, love, and security.

When your relationship with God is not in good shape, when you're unsure if you trust Him, if He's there, or even if He's good, your responses to your reality reflect that distrust, anxiety, and fear. It is only when our relationship with God is rooted in His truth, love, and goodness that we can have any hope of getting it together.

It is only when our relationship with God is rooted in His truth, love, and goodness that we can have any hope of getting it together.

CONCLUSION

YOU ONLY LIVE ONCE

Occasionally something in my current reality will trigger a memory from the past. And while my circumstances might be different, I can see how I didn't always handle things well back then. But now that I am removed from the situation, I have twenty-twenty vision. Here I am again: similar season, different times, different circumstances.

When my youngest child was in pre-K, I yearned for one thing and one thing only: kindergarten. That full day of school for her was on our horizon, and I craved it. My older three boys were already in elementary school at that point, and my daughter was going to pre-K part of the day. I had convinced myself that my life would be much more productive when all four kids were on the same schedule at the same school. Looking back, there is so much truth in that statement. But at the same time, I see now what I couldn't see then—a year of mommy-daughter time that I may never have again (or wouldn't have until she entered her junior year of high school and all her brothers were off at college). I wished away something very precious for something I thought would be better.

So now I kind of find myself here again. With my children

moving into the adult world, we're in the home stretch of having our kids in our home. In five years, this whole Ivey family thing will look very different. I've wondered what life will be like when it's just Aaron and me again, which is something we experienced for only the first two and a half years of marriage.

In these hard teenage days, I sometimes dream about and desire those future kid-free days. No dishes all over the house. No arguing over stupid stuff. No waiting up for curfew to come and go. People tell me, "Oh, you'll miss the shoes and stuff all over the house," but honestly, I don't think I will. I 100 percent know I'll miss my people—but not their stuff!

I'm having to be very disciplined. Today is the only today I ever get. When the clock strikes midnight, this day is gone, and I won't get another one of these. I don't want to waste it. I'm disciplining myself not to waste it. We shouldn't dream of and desire different days when God is giving us today.

We shouldn't dream of and desire different days when God is giving us today.

"You Only Live Once" (YOLO) rings in my ears often. When I was a crazy college kid not following Jesus, this phrase wasn't around—but boy, did I live it out! Except that my YOLO was for experiences I'd like to forget. Now as a middle-aged woman, married for two decades, raising four kids, and trying to make a mark in the world I live in, this phrase rings differently.

Ephesians 5:15–17 says, "Look carefully then how you walk, not as unwise but as wise, making the best use of the time, because the days are evil. Therefore do not be foolish, but understand what the will of the Lord is." Paul was reminding the church at Ephesus something we still need to remember today: our time matters. So many people walk around feeling out of control because they've literally lost all control of their time. Jordan Raynor says, "We are called to redeem our time because 'the days are evil' and we are running out of time to do 'the will of the Lord.'"[1]

The opportunities and gifts God has given you are unique to you, so there's no formula in this book for you to figure out what the will of the Lord is for you today. We do that by spending time in His Word, in prayer, and in community with the saints. I can't tell you what that is for you today. You have to figure that out. But I can tell you that it matters that you *do* figure it out.

We have looked at six different areas of our lives that can affect our perception of having it all together. We often feel so overwhelmed in some areas of our lives that are ultimately out of our control. In my current life I have said more times than I'd like to admit, "Jamie, get yourself together." In those moments I can choose to lean into the uncomfortable feelings, ask God to show me what I can change, and accept the things I can't, or I can continue to feel out of control. I wish I could wave a magic wand and make my life easier all the time—believe me, I would. But that's not how life works and not how we grow deeper in our love for God.

In this one life you have been given, I hope and pray that you look at the hard times, the good times, the things you can control, and the things you can't control and see that although life may be out of control, you can find a peace in the midst of it—a peace that comes only from the Father. Getting it together doesn't mean everything goes your way or even that you don't ever feel stressed. Getting it together means that your reaction to your reality comes from a place of knowing that you are deeply loved by the Father, He hasn't left you on your own, and He'll never abandon you. You might not be able to control your reality, but you can always adjust your response.

Friend, I pray you continue to chase holiness, lean into the work of the Holy Spirit in your life, access the beautiful gifts available within your community, and experience the never-ending love and grace that God has to offer you. It never runs out, and it's always waiting for you.

SCRIPTS TO MEMORIZE

So many times, we need to remind ourselves of what we already know to be true. When pondering the different aspects of your life, it will help if you have some known "scripts" ready to remind yourself of what you know to be true. These are helpful for me when I feel like life is out of control, and I hope they are also helpful for you. My hope is that you would come back to these scripts when you start to feel like you don't have it together in one of your six areas.

WHEN PONDERING MY PAST AND PRESENT HURTS:

- I am going to bring every circumstance to God because it matters to Him.
- I am going to be kind to myself.

WHEN PONDERING MY OBLIGATIONS:

- I am going to tell myself it's okay to say no.
- I am going to trust God with my plans.
- I am going to put my relationship with God first.

WHEN PONDERING MY NEEDS:

- I am going to make time to rest and care for my body.
- I am going to tell myself to see my body as a gift created by God.

WHEN PONDERING MY DESIRES:

- I am going to trust God with my desires.
- I am going to delight in God.
- I am going to pray that I would want more of God's plan and less of my own.

WHEN PONDERING MY EXPECTATIONS:

- I am going to let go of the need for perfection.
- I am going to welcome forgiveness when I fail.

WHEN PONDERING MY RESPONSIBILITIES:

- I am going to accept that I can't do it all.
- I am going to realize that comparison will steal my joy.
- I am going to view my responsibilities through the lens of the gospel.

SCRIPTURE BANK

Psalm 119 is a beautiful chapter about the benefits of Scripture in our lives. I memorized Psalm 119:105 as a child, and it's still such a source of strength and hope for me: "Your word is a lamp to my feet and a light to my path." God's Word is the guide for our lives.

Memorizing scripts to help you deal with feeling overwhelmed is great, but what I really yearn for us all to do is to hide God's Word in our hearts so that when we feel overwhelmed, these words of life will spring up in our souls and comfort us in ways nothing else ever could.

I pray that these scriptures meet you today wherever you are. God's Word is active, living, and doesn't return void.

SCRIPTURES FOR WHEN YOU'RE PONDERING YOUR PAST AND PRESENT HURTS:

- And we know that for those who love God all things work together for good, for those who are called according to his purpose. (Romans 8:28)
- "Peace I leave with you; my peace I give you. I do not give to

you as the world gives. Do not let your hearts be troubled and do not be afraid." (John 14:27 NIV)

- "Take my yoke upon you, and learn from me, for I am gentle and lowly in heart, and you will find rest for your souls." (Matthew 11:29)
- "I am the vine; you are the branches. Whoever abides in me and I in him, he it is that bears much fruit, for apart from me you can do nothing." (John 15:5)
- You have kept count of my tossings; put my tears in your bottle. Are they not in your book? (Psalm 56:8)

SCRIPTURES FOR WHEN YOU'RE PONDERING YOUR OBLIGATIONS:

- Now as they went on their way, Jesus entered a village. And a woman named Martha welcomed him into her house. And she had a sister called Mary, who sat at the Lord's feet and listened to his teaching. But Martha was distracted with much serving. And she went up to him and said, "Lord, do you not care that my sister has left me to serve alone? Tell her then to help me." But the Lord answered her, "Martha, Martha, you are anxious and troubled about many things, but one thing is necessary. Mary has chosen the good portion, which will not be taken away from her." (Luke 10:38–42)
- For we are his workmanship, created in Christ Jesus for good works, which God prepared beforehand, that we should walk in them. (Ephesians 2:10)
- Present yourselves to God as those who have been brought from death to life, and your members to God as instruments for righteousness. (Romans 6:13)

- He died for all, that those who live might no longer live for themselves but for him who for their sake died and was raised. (2 Corinthians 5:15)

SCRIPTURES FOR WHEN YOU'RE PONDERING YOUR NEEDS:

- "Look at the birds of the air: they neither sow nor reap nor gather into barns, and yet your heavenly Father feeds them. Are you not of more value than they? And which of you by being anxious can add a single hour to his span of life? And why are you anxious about clothing? Consider the lilies of the field, how they grow: they neither toil nor spin, yet I tell you, even Solomon in all his glory was not arrayed like one of these. But if God so clothes the grass of the field, which today is alive and tomorrow is thrown into the oven, will he not much more clothe you?" (Matthew 6:26–30)
- [Jesus] emptied himself, by taking the form of a servant, being born in the likeness of men. (Philippians 2:7)
- Do you not know that your body is a temple of the Holy Spirit within you, whom you have from God? You are not your own, for you were bought with a price. So glorify God in your body. (1 Corinthians 6:19–20)
- I praise you, for I am fearfully and wonderfully made. Wonderful are your works; my soul knows it very well. (Psalm 139:14)

SCRIPTURES FOR WHEN YOU'RE PONDERING YOUR DESIRES:

- And going a little farther he fell on his face and prayed, saying, "My Father, if it be possible, let this cup pass from me;

nevertheless, not as I will, but as you will." . . . Again, for the second time, he went away and prayed, "My Father, if this cannot pass unless I drink it, your will be done." (Matthew 26:39, 42)

- For it is God who works in you, both to will and to work for his good pleasure. (Philippians 2:13)
- Many are the plans in the mind of a man, but it is the purpose of the LORD that will stand. (Proverbs 19:21)
- Delight yourself in the LORD, and he will give you the desires of your heart. (Psalm 37:4)
- "Whatever you ask in my name, this I will do, that the Father may be glorified in the Son." (John 14:13)

SCRIPTURES FOR WHEN YOU'RE PONDERING YOUR EXPECTATIONS:

- Peter answered him, "Though they all fall away because of you, I will never fall away." Jesus said to him, "Truly, I tell you, this very night, before the rooster crows, you will deny me three times." Peter said to him, "Even if I must die with you, I will not deny you!" And all the disciples said the same. . . . And Peter remembered the saying of Jesus, "Before the rooster crows, you will deny me three times." And he went out and wept bitterly. (Matthew 26:33–35, 75)
- Weeping may stay overnight, but there is joy in the morning (Psalm 30:5 CSB)
- My soul, wait silently for God alone, for my expectation is from Him. (Psalm 62:5 NKJV)
- Do not be anxious about anything, but in everything by prayer and supplication with thanksgiving let your requests be made known to God. (Philippians 4:6)

SCRIPTURES FOR WHEN YOU'RE PONDERING YOUR RESPONSIBILITIES:

- Your eyes saw my unformed substance; in your book were written, every one of them, the days that were formed for me, when as yet there was none of them. (Psalm 139:16)
- "Come to me, all who labor and are heavy laden, and I will give you rest." (Matthew 11:28)
- Each of you should use whatever gift you have received to serve others, as faithful stewards of God's grace in its various forms. (1 Peter 4:10 NIV)
- For this is the love of God, that we keep his commandments. And his commandments are not burdensome. (1 John 5:3)
- Now to him who is able to do far more abundantly than all that we ask or think, according to the power at work within us, to him be glory in the church and in Christ Jesus throughout all generations. (Ephesians 3:20–21)

ACKNOWLEDGMENTS

This book is in your hands because of many people who not only believed in me and this project but poured their hearts into it as well. The entire team at W, I barely have words for the way you have stewarded this message and me as an author. When I was picking the publishing team to partner with for this book, what drew me to W was a sense that the gospel of Jesus Christ was at the center of everything you did. I want that to be said about my life. Partnering with y'all has been a joy. Damon, thank you for believing in me. Stephanie, thanks for guiding me. Everyone on the team—this book is better because of you. Thank you.

Writing a book is truly the best group project ever. Jenni, you advocate for me and believe in me so well. Lysa, your inspiration helped shape this book into what it is today. Lindsey, thank you for your help in putting the words on these pages. Lyndsey, thanks for the way you cheered me on and spoke into this project.

Thank you to my husband, Aaron, who believes in me more than anyone should. My kids, I hope that it's not my words that make you proud of me but my life. You five are my greatest joys; thank you for the sacrifices you all make so I can do what I do.

ACKNOWLEDGMENTS

Jesus, You continue to shape me into the woman You want me to be. I give You these words and my life—use them for Your glory and Your glory alone.

NOTES

Introduction

1. "God I Look to You" from Bethel Music—get it in your ears ASAP!

Chapter 1

1. Tyler David, "The Pursuit of Wisdom: Wisdom in Decision Making," The Austin Stone Community Church, Austin, TX, June 15, 2014, www.austinstone.org/sermons/wisdom-in-decision-making.

Chapter 2

1. Angie Smith, *Woven: Understanding the Bible as One Seamless Story* (Nashville: B&H Publishing, 2021), 24.
2. "Center My Life," written by Aaron Ivey and Brett Land.

Chapter 4

1. Alicia Britt Chole, *Anonymous: Jesus' Hidden Years . . . and Yours* (Nashville: Thomas Nelson, 2011), 15.
2. Beth Moore, *All My Knotted-Up Life: A Memoir* (Carol Stream, IL: Tyndale House, 2023), 80.
3. Chris Cleave, *Little Bee* (New York: Simon & Schuster, 2008), 9.
4. Alison Cook, *Boundaries for Your Soul: How to Turn Your Overwhelming Thoughts and Feelings into Your Greatest Allies* (Nashville: Thomas Nelson, 2018), 43.
5. Curt Thompson, *Anatomy of the Soul: Surprising Connections between Neuroscience and Spiritual Practices That Can Transform Your Life and Relationships* (Carol Stream, IL: Tyndale House, 2010), 47.

6. Kat Armstrong, *Valleys: Finding Courage, Conviction, and Confidence in Life's Low Points* (Carol Stream, IL: NavPress, 2023), 30.

7. "Happy Hour #278: Beth Moore," January 1, 2020, in *The Happy Hour with Jamie Ivey*, podcast, www.jamieivey.com/278-beth-moore.

8. Mary Marantz (@marymarantz), "There is this version of you that you became in order to survive," Instagram, April 20, 2023, www.instagram.com/marymarantz.

Chapter 5

1. Jeanne Stevens, *What's Here Now: How to Stop Rehashing the Past and Rehearsing the Future—and Start Receiving the Present* (Grand Rapids, MI: Revell, 2022), 148.

Chapter 6

1. Jess Connolly, *Breaking Free from Body Shame: Dare to Reclaim What God Has Named Good* (Grand Rapids, MI: Zondervan, 2021), 6.

2. Rebekah Lyons, *Rhythms of Renewal: Trading Stress and Anxiety for a Life of Peace and Purpose* (Grand Rapids, MI: Zondervan, 2019), 13.

3. Saundra Dalton-Smith, "Working from a Place of Rest," *Jesus Calling* (blog), accessed June 5, 2023, www.jesuscalling.com/blog/working-from-a-place-of-rest.

Chapter 7

1. Curt Thompson, *The Soul of Desire: Discovering the Neuroscience of Longing, Beauty, and Community* (Downers Grove, IL: InterVarsity Press, 2021).

2. David Platt, *Radical: Taking Back Your Faith from the American Dream* (Colorado Springs: Multnomah, 2010), 181.

3. See, for example, "Day 001: Genesis 1–3," December 31, 2022, in *The Bible Recap*, podcast, www.thebiblerecap.com/podcast.

4. Tim Chaffey, "Would Joseph's Family Shun Mary?", Answers in Genesis, December 31, 2010, https://answersingenesis.org/christmas/would-josephs-family-shun-mary.

ABOUT THE AUTHOR

Since 2014 when Jamie launched her podcast, *The Happy Hour with Jamie Ivey*, she has been elevating the stories of women and men chasing hard after Jesus. She believes that stories change the world, and that belief has been her motivation as Jamie has fostered a community of listeners eager to hear from others with different life experiences or unique perspectives. On *The Happy Hour*, Jamie and a guest discuss the big things in life, the little things in life, and everything in between. In every podcast episode, listeners are pointed to Jesus, and it's a joy for Jamie to be the one behind the microphone bringing these stories to life.

Jamie has previously written books from a place of wanting women specifically to find their worth in Christ alone and pursue contentment in where God has specifically placed them. She considers it a great privilege to write books based on what the Lord has already done in her own heart, and this book is no different. Jamie has fought against the lie that everyone else has it together and she is lacking or falling behind. The truth is, none of us do. Only in looking to Jesus and the life He lived perfectly can we find true freedom from the unrealistic expectations we put on ourselves.

Jamie lives in Austin, Texas, with her husband, Aaron; their four children; and two dogs. She loves college football and her newfound love of walking as a spiritual discipline, and she remains committed to trying every new restaurant in her foodie town.

Chapter 9

1. Ann Voskamp (@AnnVoskamp), "Being joyful isn't what makes you grateful," X, October 9, 2014, 6:45 P.M., x.com/AnnVoskamp/status /520359318084804608.
2. Chole, *Anonymous*, 9.
3. "The Happy Hour #544: Characters of Christmas (Mary) with Jami Nato," December 2, 2022, in *The Happy Hour with Jamie Ivey*, podcast, www.jamieivey.com/hh544.

Chapter 10

1. Jackie Hill Perry, *Holier Than Thou: How God's Holiness Helps Us Trust Him* (Nashville: B&H Books, 2021), 15.
2. "Episode 419: Rethinking Roe, Crotch Christianity, and Militant Masculinity with Kristin Kobes Du Mez," August 26, 2020, in *Holy Post*, podcast, www.holypost.com/post/episode-419-rethinking-roe -crotch-christianity-militant-masculinity-with-kristin-kobes-du-mez.
3. "The Happy Hour #428: Jackie Hill Perry," September 24, 2021, in *The Happy Hour with Jamie Ivey*, podcast, www.jamieivey.com/the -happy-hour-jackie-hill-perry.
4. Hill Perry, *Holier Than Thou*.
5. "The Happy Hour #428: Jackie Hill Perry."

Chapter 11

1. Roy Ratcliff, *Dark Journey Deep Grace: Jeffrey Dahmer's Story of Faith* (Abilene, TX: Leafwood Publishers, 2006), 84.
2. Bryan Stevenson, *Just Mercy: A Story of Justice and Redemption* (New York: Random House, 2014), 17.
3. Timothy Keller, *Romans 1–7 for You* (Charlotte, NC: Good Book Company, 2014), 170.
4. Keller, *Romans 1–7 for You*, 169.
5. Tim Chester, *You Can Change: God's Transforming Power for Our Sinful Behavior and Negative Emotions* (Wheaton, IL: Crossway, 2010), 74.
6. Keller, *Romans 1–7 for You*, 171.

7. Jeanne Stevens, *What's Here Now? How to Stop Rehashing the Past and Rehearsing the Future—and Start Receiving the Present* (Grand Rapids, MI: Baker, 2022), 57.

8. Timothy Keller, *Romans 8–16 for You* (Charlotte, NC: Good Book Company, 2015), 12.

9. Cited in Keller, *Romans 8–16 for You*, 13–14.

Chapter 12

1. Chester, *You Can Change*, 163.

2. Chester, *You Can Change*, 156.

3. Thompson, *Anatomy of the Soul*, 155.

4. Chester, *You Can Change*, 153.

5. Jennie Allen, *Find Your People: Building Deep Community in a Lonely World* (Colorado Springs: WaterBrook, 2022), 134.

6. Debra Fileta (@debrafileta), "Feelings (even the worst ones) aren't a sin, they're a signal," Instagram, January 12, 2023, www.instagram.com/p/CnU9hr1SPbi.

7. Cited in Joseph Rhea, "Bring Your Sin into the Light," Gospel Coalition, February 15, 2021, www.thegospelcoalition.org/article/bring-sin-light.

Chapter 13

1. John Eldredge, *Resilient: Restoring Your Weary Soul in These Turbulent Times* (Nashville: Thomas Nelson, 2022), 157.

2. "The Serenity Prayer," attributed to Reinhold Niebuhr.

3. Paraphrased from Jo March in Louisa May Alcott, *Little Women*.

Chapter 14

1. C. John Collins, "Introduction to the Psalms," in ESV *Study Bible* (Wheaton, IL: Crossway, 2008), 935.

2. "The Happy Hour #189: Tova Sido," April 18, 2018, in *The Happy Hour with Jamie Ivey*, podcast, www.jamieivey.com/the-happy-hour-189-tova-sido.

3. "Another in the Fire," words and music by Chris Davenport and Joel Houston, Hillsong United, 2018.

Conclusion

1. Jordan Raynor, *Redeeming Your Time: Seven Biblical Principles for Being Purposeful, Present, and Wildly Productive* (Colorado Springs: WaterBrook, 2021), xxiii.

Chapter 9

1. Ann Voskamp (@AnnVoskamp), "Being joyful isn't what makes you grateful," X, October 9, 2014, 6:45 P.M., x.com/AnnVoskamp/status /520359318084804608.
2. Chole, *Anonymous*, 9.
3. "The Happy Hour #544: Characters of Christmas (Mary) with Jami Nato," December 2, 2022, in *The Happy Hour with Jamie Ivey*, podcast, www.jamieivey.com/hh544.

Chapter 10

1. Jackie Hill Perry, *Holier Than Thou: How God's Holiness Helps Us Trust Him* (Nashville: B&H Books, 2021), 15.
2. "Episode 419: Rethinking Roe, Crotch Christianity, and Militant Masculinity with Kristin Kobes Du Mez," August 26, 2020, in *Holy Post*, podcast, www.holypost.com/post/episode-419-rethinking-roe -crotch-christianity-militant-masculinity-with-kristin-kobes-du-mez.
3. "The Happy Hour #428: Jackie Hill Perry," September 24, 2021, in *The Happy Hour with Jamie Ivey*, podcast, www.jamieivey.com/the -happy-hour-jackie-hill-perry.
4. Hill Perry, *Holier Than Thou*.
5. "The Happy Hour #428: Jackie Hill Perry."

Chapter 11

1. Roy Ratcliff, *Dark Journey Deep Grace: Jeffrey Dahmer's Story of Faith* (Abilene, TX: Leafwood Publishers, 2006), 84.
2. Bryan Stevenson, *Just Mercy: A Story of Justice and Redemption* (New York: Random House, 2014), 17.
3. Timothy Keller, *Romans 1–7 for You* (Charlotte, NC: Good Book Company, 2014), 170.
4. Keller, *Romans 1–7 for You*, 169.
5. Tim Chester, *You Can Change: God's Transforming Power for Our Sinful Behavior and Negative Emotions* (Wheaton, IL: Crossway, 2010), 74.
6. Keller, *Romans 1–7 for You*, 171.

7. Jeanne Stevens, *What's Here Now? How to Stop Rehashing the Past and Rehearsing the Future—and Start Receiving the Present* (Grand Rapids, MI: Baker, 2022), 57.

8. Timothy Keller, *Romans 8–16 for You* (Charlotte, NC: Good Book Company, 2015), 12.

9. Cited in Keller, *Romans 8–16 for You*, 13–14.

Chapter 12

1. Chester, *You Can Change*, 163.

2. Chester, *You Can Change*, 156.

3. Thompson, *Anatomy of the Soul*, 155.

4. Chester, *You Can Change*, 153.

5. Jennie Allen, *Find Your People: Building Deep Community in a Lonely World* (Colorado Springs: WaterBrook, 2022), 134.

6. Debra Fileta (@debrafileta), "Feelings (even the worst ones) aren't a sin, they're a signal," Instagram, January 12, 2023, www.instagram .com/p/CnU9hr1SPbi.

7. Cited in Joseph Rhea, "Bring Your Sin into the Light," Gospel Coalition, February 15, 2021, www.thegospelcoalition.org/article /bring-sin-light.

Chapter 13

1. John Eldredge, *Resilient: Restoring Your Weary Soul in These Turbulent Times* (Nashville: Thomas Nelson, 2022), 157.

2. "The Serenity Prayer," attributed to Reinhold Niebuhr.

3. Paraphrased from Jo March in Louisa May Alcott, *Little Women*.

Chapter 14

1. C. John Collins, "Introduction to the Psalms," in ESV *Study Bible* (Wheaton, IL: Crossway, 2008), 935.

2. "The Happy Hour #189: Tova Sido," April 18, 2018, in *The Happy Hour with Jamie Ivey*, podcast, www.jamieivey.com/the-happy -hour-189-tova-sido.

3. "Another in the Fire," words and music by Chris Davenport and Joel Houston, Hillsong United, 2018.

Conclusion

1. Jordan Raynor, *Redeeming Your Time: Seven Biblical Principles for Being Purposeful, Present, and Wildly Productive* (Colorado Springs: WaterBrook, 2021), xxiii.

ABOUT THE AUTHOR

Since 2014 when Jamie launched her podcast, *The Happy Hour with Jamie Ivey*, she has been elevating the stories of women and men chasing hard after Jesus. She believes that stories change the world, and that belief has been her motivation as Jamie has fostered a community of listeners eager to hear from others with different life experiences or unique perspectives. On *The Happy Hour*, Jamie and a guest discuss the big things in life, the little things in life, and everything in between. In every podcast episode, listeners are pointed to Jesus, and it's a joy for Jamie to be the one behind the microphone bringing these stories to life.

Jamie has previously written books from a place of wanting women specifically to find their worth in Christ alone and pursue contentment in where God has specifically placed them. She considers it a great privilege to write books based on what the Lord has already done in her own heart, and this book is no different. Jamie has fought against the lie that everyone else has it together and she is lacking or falling behind. The truth is, none of us do. Only in looking to Jesus and the life He lived perfectly can we find true freedom from the unrealistic expectations we put on ourselves.

Jamie lives in Austin, Texas, with her husband, Aaron; their four children; and two dogs. She loves college football and her newfound love of walking as a spiritual discipline, and she remains committed to trying every new restaurant in her foodie town.